Left: Shiraz Tal demonstrates the impact of a single cutout and a gold ornament in an otherwise minimalist gown. Long white viscose dress, Gucci, $1,395.
Right: An off-center strap and a single drop earring skew the usual symmetry. Black viscose-and-rayon jersey dress, Calvin Klein, $1,240. For details, see Shopping Guide. Hair, Didier Malige for Frederic Fekkai Beauté; makeup, Fran Cooper for the Stephen Knoll Salon; fashion editor, Jon Moore.

■ **BEAUTYWATCH** Variations on a theme: Hairstylist Didier Malige used Pantene Pro-V Spray-On Gel to take slicked-back hair from a sleek updo to a side-swept pompadour.

CHANEL

THE COUTURIERE AT WORK

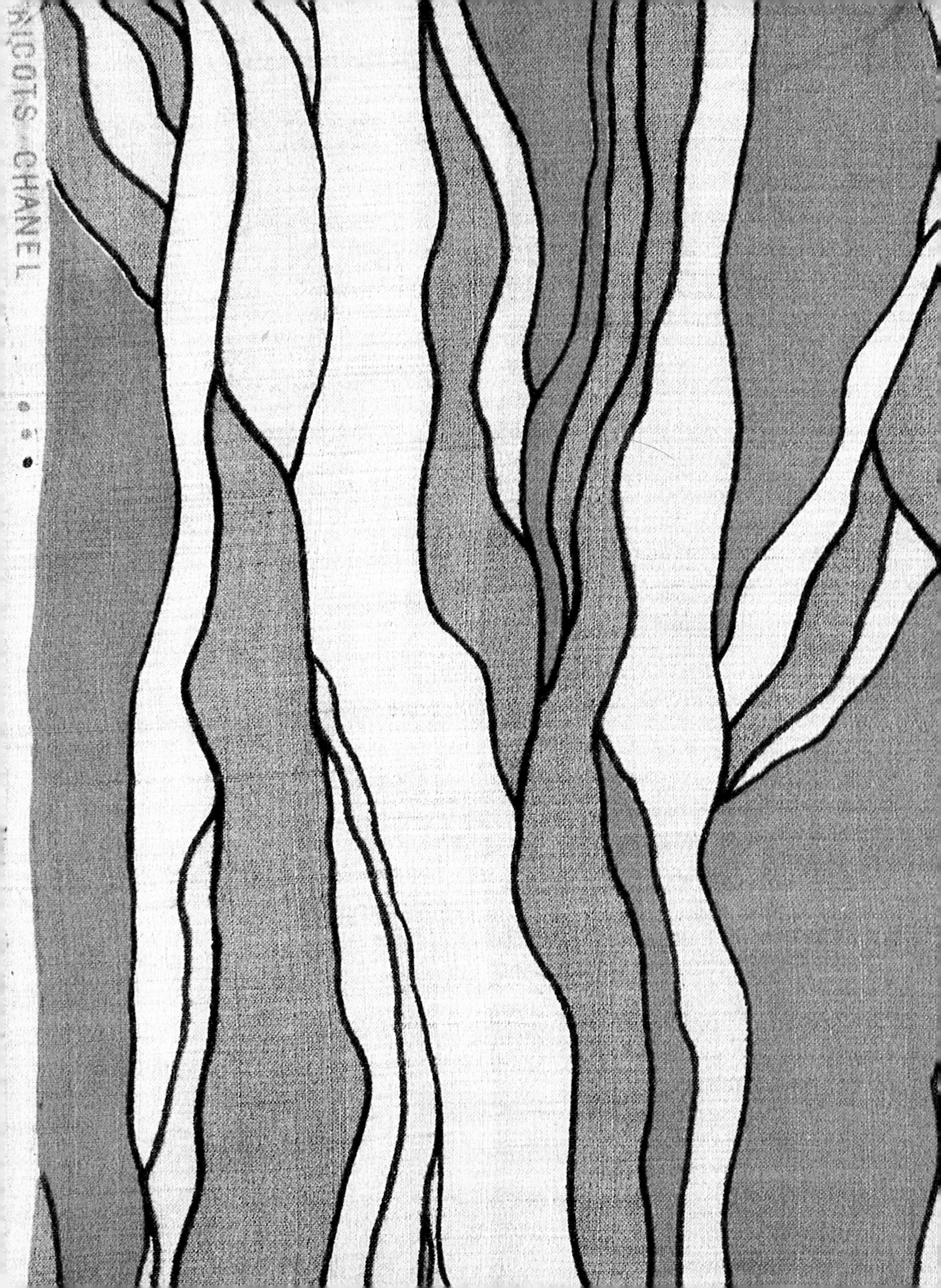
RICOTS CHANEL

CHANEL

THE COUTURIERE AT WORK

AMY DE LA HAYE, SHELLEY TOBIN

The Overlook Press
Woodstock • New York

Acknowledgments

The authors would like to thank many colleagues for help during the
preparation of this book.

Karl Lagerfeld and, at Chanel in Paris, Marie-Louise de Clermont Tonnerre,
Veronique Perez, Sophie Lorthiois and, in particular, Bernadette Rendall whose
kindness and patience never wavered. Also, Louise Brassey at Chanel, London,
whose enthusiasm and assistance were also greatly appreciated.

Tracy Allen and Alison Carter of the Hampshire Museum Service. Diane Moss
of the Pickford's House Museum in Derby. Don Petrillo of the Fashion Institute of
Technology, New York. Kimberley Fink of the Costume Institute. Metropolitan
Museum of Art, New York. Valerie Guillaume of the Musée de la Mode et du
Costume, Paris.

In the Victoria & Albert Museum, Valerie Mendes, Gillian Varley and Avril Hart.
Lesley Burton, Jennifer Blain and John Taylor of V&A Publications and staff in the
Photo Studio and Picture Library.

Cara Gallardo and Richard Smith of the designers, Area. Niall McInerney
for the use of contemporary catwalk photographs.

First paperback published in the
United States in 1996 by
The Overlook Press
Lewis Hollow Road
Woodstock, New York 12498

Library of Congress Cataloging-in-Publication
Data

De La Haye, Amy
Chanel, the couturière at work / Amy De La
Haye, Shelly Tobin. p.ca.
Includes bibliographical references and index.
1. Costume design – France – History – 20th
Century
2. Chanel, Coco, 1883-1971. I. Tobin, Shelly.
II. Title.
TT507.D4 1994
746.9'2'092--dc20
94-27235
CIP·

Printed by Grafiche Milani, Italy

ISBN: 0-87951-639-9

First Printing

Frontispiece: Chanel's printed
dress silk, 1929

This abstract design was
registered at the Manchester
Design Registry (number
272017) to protect the design
from being copied by textile
manufacturers. It would also
have been registered in
France. In the selvedge is
printed Tissus Chanel, the
name of Chanel's French
textile factory.

Victoria & Albert Museum,
London (T.192-1975)

CONTENTS

One THE FOUNDATIONS OF THE CHANEL EMPIRE

Sem (Georges Goursat)
Tangoville sur Mer, 1913

The tango, a dance of South American origin, began in the United States in 1911, and soon became all the rage in Europe. Here the caricaturist represents Chanel the milliner, hat box on arm, dancing with Boy Capel as a polo-playing centaur. A small feathered hat dangles from the end of his polo mallet. Chanel is still wearing the long straight skirt fitting tight to the ankles from which she was soon to liberate fashionable women. Chanel's Deauville shop opened in 1913, and this caricature sums up the latest interests of fashionable society, placing Chanel at the centre of it.

EARLY LIFE

Gabrielle Chanel was born in the French town of Saumur in the Loire valley on 19 August 1883, the second daughter of Albert Chanel, an itinerant salesman, and Jeanne Devolle. The birth was registered at the local *mairie*, witnessed by poorhouse employees. The name on the birth certificate was misspelt Chasnel. When the world knew her as Coco, the celebrated couturière, Gabrielle Chanel, the woman whose name was to become synonymous with style, preferred to 'forget' her origins, which has caused problems for researchers ever since.

Jeanne and Albert were married on 17 November 1884, but Jeanne suffered from ill health and Gabrielle was later to paint a romantic picture of her mother succumbing to consumption at the age of 32. Albert was left alone with five children, Julia, Gabrielle, Alphonse, Antoinette and Lucien. He was incapable of looking after them so in 1895, when Gabrielle was 12 years old, her brothers were sent to work on a farm and the girls were sent to an orphanage run by the sisters of the Congregation of the Sacred Heart of Mary at Aubazine near Brive-la-Gaillarde in the Corrèze region. In the holidays the girls were able to escape the austerity of the orphanage to stay with their grandparents in the garrison town of Moulins near Vichy in central France. In 1900 Chanel moved there permanently and for the next two years attended a local convent school with her aunt Adrienne who was nearly her own age and was to remain a valued friend.

Moulins was said at that time to be the most popular cavalry garrison in France. Local businesses catered for the needs of the young officers stationed in the town. Gabrielle and Adrienne had been taught to sew at the convent and with these skills were able to find work as dressmakers. Adrienne had started work as an assistant for Monsieur Henri Desboutin, whose shop, the House of Grampayre, sold lingerie, linen and hosiery and, with a recommendation from the Mother Superior, Gabrielle was able to join her.

Even though her first employment was connected with clothes, Chanel's earliest ambition was to appear on the stage. The fashionable entertainment of the day, the *café concerts*, were in plentiful supply at Moulins and well attended by young officers. Several sources maintain that the famous nickname 'Coco' was derived from Chanel's version of a popular song about a young lady from Paris who has lost her dog, *Qui qu'a vu Coco?* Whatever the reason, soon she was known to her fans in the audience as 'la petite Coco'. This love of limelight was to reappear constantly in her later life.

No-one seems exactly sure how Gabrielle first met Etienne Balsan. Chanel's biographer, Axel Madsen, notes that they probably met when Chanel worked on Sunday mornings as a tailor's assistant at a shop frequented by dandy young officers in search of the smartest uniform.

Balsan was the youngest son of a family which had built its fortune on textiles and, like Chanel, he was an orphan. He was a handsome figure and a rich man, having received an inheritance from both his father, who died in 1896, and his mother, who died six years later. Educated in England, he developed a passion for horse racing, training horses and taking part in races for 'gentlemen' riders. He chose not to continue the family tradition, using his wealth to acquire the estate near Compiègne in 1904. It was ideal for his purposes as a breeder and trainer, also being close to Chantilly with its racecourse, and was already established as a centre of equestrian activity. Meanwhile, Balsan's brothers, Jacques and Robert, continued to expand the family business based in the wool town of Châteauroux.

Gabrielle was about 25 when she went to live with Balsan and her association with him and with his rich and cultured friends did much to help Chanel break with the past life she despised. According to François Calame, writing in the catalogue of an exhibition at the Abbaye de Royallieu, local census returns for 1906 show that Gabrielle Chanel, *sans profession*, was already a resident on the vast Balsan estate. Although she is listed among the many other inhabitants, including grooms, jockeys and servants, it is significant that her name directly follows the entry for Etienne Balsan, *entraîneur* (horse-trainer).

THE FOUNDATIONS OF THE CHANEL EMPIRE

At his estate La Croix-Saint-Ouen Balsan pursued pleasure and sport, entertaining actresses and *demi-mondaines*. He had already installed one mistress there. She was

Fashion Photographs by Seeberger Frères, c.1909

(Above, left) By 1909, the revival of the French directoire style influenced dresses such as this high-waisted gown. Fussy draperies and elaborate trimmings and accessories hampered movement, the enormous top-heavy hat shown here contrasts with the elegant lines of those by Chanel which she dressed with a single plume as opposed to what appears to be the feathers of an entire bird. The writer Aldous Huxley described such a hat in *Eyeless in Gaza* as 'a French funeral of the first class'.

Like Chanel, Paul Poiret was of humble origins. He also began his career designing for actresses. As an employee of Jacques Doucet he made a cape for one of Doucet's most valued clients, the actress Réjane. The theatre emulated society and vice versa – actresses collaborated with the couturiers to mutual benefit. This voluminous satin cloak with decorative embroidery is by Poiret, it was photographed by Seeberger Frères whose work appeared in the pages of many fashion magazines.

Emilienne d'Alençon, a celebrated courtesan. Chanel's reaction to this arrangement has never been referred to in detail, and it is difficult to define her position in Balsan's household at this time.

Chanel's contemporaries admired her spirit and accomplishment as a horsewoman. The young woman's love of horses helped to distance her from the role of *irregulière* which, with her lowly beginnings, would have prevented her from being accepted into society. However, she was observant and she effectively dissociated herself from these women in her demeanour and attire, while carefully marking the strict rules governing social conduct.

In contrast to the ostentatious status dressing prevalent at the time, Chanel preferred simple costumes. Her appearance was modest and neat. She later reminisced that on arrival at Balsan's estate her wardrobe consisted only of an alpaca suit for the summer, a cheviot suit for the winter, and a goatskin jacket. To Marcel Haedrich she confided that her suits had their origins in a tailored costume she wore during her teens. Chanel's plain tailor-mades and small hats must have appeared eccentric compared to the attire of the courtesans, lavishly decked out in frills and furbelows and just as lavishly made-up and perfumed. Perhaps not surprisingly, her mission in due course became that of abolishing the obviously complicated and unnecessarily extravagant in dress.

Chanel had the tailor at La Croix-Saint-Ouen make her suitable riding clothes. Although it was more usual for women at the time to ride side-saddle, it was now customary for women to wear a 'safety' skirt over breeches with a tailored jacket (traditional English tailoring was greatly admired and specialist outfitters catered for equestrian sports), Chanel was a modern sportswoman. When she went riding with the men at first light she rode astride. Surviving photographs show Chanel at the stables dressed in jodhpurs and a shirt with a small collar and – another mannish touch – a knitted tie. Indeed her clothes are not so very different from those worn by her male companions. Many of the stable-hands and jockeys employed by Balsan were British, and the stables may represent Chanel's first contact with British sporting dress.

Chanel herself later claimed to have taken the riding jacket as an example for her own subsequent creations and remarked that the local tailor inspired all her models. She often favoured masculine styles, elements of which were to survive even into her final collections, in particular the small boater-shaped hats, neat collars, and shirt cuffs fastened with cuff-links.

Photographs of this period (some are reproduced in Charles Roux) show Chanel in tailor-made jacket and skirt or clothes for sport, and there is a series of pictures depicting play-acting a country wedding, where Chanel is dressed as best man, with clothes presumably lent by men in the party. However, just one photograph showing her in more obviously feminine attire survives. Dated to 1909, when Chanel would have been 26, this shows her in a simple V-necked dress with lace under-bodice trimmed with ribbon.

In 1907, Chanel met the wealthy English businessman, Arthur 'Boy' Capel. His interests in Newcastle coal-mines and shipping were to make him a millionaire during the First World War. He was a fine polo player and fitted in well with the Balsan set. Life continued to revolve around horses, women and the occasional game.

THE MILLINER

Chanel had a flair for trimming hats. Already in the habit of modifying her own shop-bought hats, she was soon in demand by Balsan's visitors. She used to buy basic straw boaters and hats from the Galeries Lafayette department store in Paris and trim them herself. But these were not the overly fussy, plumed and beribboned affairs which created the top-heavy look that was generally the fashion at the time. Chanel's hats

Gabrielle Dorziat wearing a hat by Gabrielle Chanel, 1912.

Dorziat was a successful, well-known actress and became a friend of Chanel. This photograph appeared in the May edition of the magazine *Les Modes* in 1912. By this time Chanel's name had become as well-known as those of the stars of the Paris stage for whom she created her chic and stylish hats. The actress Lucienne Roger was first featured in a Chanel hat on the cover of *Comoedia Illustrée* in Autumn 1910. Chanel's business address is given as 21 rue Cambon. *Comoedia Illustrée* published stories and reviews relating to the contemporary stage, and regularly reported on the clothes worn by its fashionable stars. Photographs of Chanel hats featured in subsequent issues of the magazine, and were shown every month from September through to January 1911. Chanel even appeared modelling her own creations in the October 1910 issue. Her hats appeared as accessories to dresses by Paquin and Doucet, and were acclaimed for their unfailing good taste and stylish lines. Dorziat was so faithful to her *modiste* that she rushed to the rue Cambon the moment she returned from a successful tour to St Petersburg.

were simply trimmed and worn perfectly straight. It seems likely that Emilienne d'Alençon may have brought Chanel to public attention when she wore one of her hats to the races. By this time, Emilienne had taken up with the celebrated jockey Alec Carter, and had become the darling of the gossip columns. Encouraged by this success, and perhaps with a view to her future security, Chanel asked Balsan to set her up in a Paris shop. When he refused, she persuaded him to let her move to Paris and use his apartment at 160 Boulevard Malesherbes, where she employed a professional milliner and later her sister Antoinette and two assistants. This enterprise began around 1908-9.

In Paris, the relationship between Boy and Chanel grew deeper than friendship. Chanel lived with Boy on the Avenue Gabriel and the couple went out every evening to the opera, Maxim's or the Café de Paris. Despite the fact that their liaison was frowned upon in certain quarters, Chanel was fascinated by Parisian society. Commerce was Boy's world and the entrepreneur in him probably recognised Chanel's ambition and was confident of her intelligence, energy and business sense. As she had no money, he generously agreed to advance money to enable her to rent commercial premises on the rue Cambon, centre of the already well-established couture industry. Chanel was later to comment that Capel was as important to her as her whole family: 'He made me what I am, developed what was unique in me, to the exclusion of the rest'. (Leymarie, p.47).

Although the business did not bring in profits immediately, it was to be the foundation of an empire. Chanel Modes opened at 21 rue Cambon in about 1910. The original lease of the property stated that Chanel had no right to make dresses there as a dressmaker was already working in the building, so initially she worked solely as a milliner.

The years 1911 and 1912 were to be good ones for Chanel. Chanel Modes received enthusiastic reviews in magazines, with illustrations of Chanel's models being worn by the favourite actresses of the day. She was even featured modelling her hats herself in *Comoedia Illustrée*, Autumn 1910. The cover illustration showed actress Lucienne Roger wearing a Chanel hat decked with a bird of paradise, clearly crediting her with its creation and noting the address, 21 rue Cambon.

Sem (Georges Goursat)

Mam'selle Coco, j'voudrais un beau chapeau pour le Dimanche, 1914

Chanel simply-dressed in shirt and skirt offers hats to her customer. The hats are less cluttered than those of previous years.

„Mam'selle Coco j'voudrais un
beau chapeau pour le Dimanche"

Gabrielle Dorziat, an actress whom Chanel already knew, was to play the leading role at the Théâtre de Vaudeville in a play based on a story by Guy de Maupassant. Her wardrobe was by Jacques Doucet and Chanel supplied the hats. Doucet was head of an old-established couture house and a favourite of both the actress Réjane and Emilienne d'Alençon. Dorziat was photographed in *Journal des Modes*, 12 May 1912 wearing two of the wide-brimmed straw hats with brims upturned to one side. *Les Modes* also showed full-page photographs of Chanel hats worn by both Dorziat and another famous actress, Geneviève Vix. The illustrator Paul Iribe, with whom Chanel became deeply involved in the 1930s (see page 70), also drew his then wife, the actress Jeanne Dirys, in one of her hats for the same journal.

Chanel's style was a reaction to the blowsiness of the Belle Epoque. Gradually society women, like the Comtesse de Gontaut-Biron, daughter of the American ambassador to Germany, joined the actresses and *cocottes* as Chanel's clients, fascinated by her unconventionality. Chanel's success with hats and her strong opinions about contemporary fashion led her to set her own style. Her customers responded by asking her to copy dresses from her own wardrobe for them, but there is no evidence to show exactly when she first ventured into dressmaking.

With business brisk on the rue Cambon, Boy no longer needed to secure her loan with the bank. Chanel was often quoted as saying that money held no interest for her, her only concern being to gain independence. By 1913 she had achieved this aim.

FASHION BACKGROUND

When Chanel was employed around 1903 at the Desboutin shop in Moulins, selling silks, lace and ribbons, feathers, furs and trimmings, the Paris couture houses of Worth, Paquin and Doucet were already dressing the fashionable world. Their creations were publicised in women's fashion magazines such as *Les Modes* , which featured photographs of celebrity models, actresses and singers wearing the latest confections. In the early years of the 20th century periodicals employed photographers and gossip writers who covered the seasonal rounds of sporting and other fashionable events. Their cameras captured the elaborate fashions of the day. The world of the actress and *demi-monde* were quite closely connected. Actresses such as Réjane, who was exclusively dressed by Doucet, were used as models by couturiers and regularly appeared in, and even on the cover of, fashion magazines with a wealthy and exclusive readership.

The 'S'-bend corset, with its rigid vertical boning, straight front and moulded waist, had the effect of thrusting the bosom forward and the hips backwards, balancing the tiny waist with rounded curves and skirts sweeping towards the hem. An abundance of trimmings completed the effect. Lace and feathers were used in quantity, with beading and sequins popular additions for *décolleté* evening gowns. By contrast, day dresses were equipped with high-standing collars, the fineness of the materials often belying the rigid boned structure underneath. Favourite colours were pale pastel blues and roses, eau-de-nil, white and cream, with black and midnight blue appearing for evening. Materials were correspondingly light and delicate: fragile gauzes and chiffons, filmy *mousselines de soie* and tulles over silks and satins.

Etiquette demanded a correct outfit for every occasion, with as many as six changes of clothing a day. Getting dressed was a complicated business and caring for the garments time-consuming and expensive, a task which fell to the lady's maid who had to grapple with the fiddly hook-and-eye fastenings and spend hours crimping chiffon frills and flounces back into shape.

However, women were also beginning to adopt suitable clothing for going out to work and for active sports. Tailor-made walking costumes in woollen cloths were often styled along masculine lines, as was dress for sports such as golf. The increasing popularity of motoring also introduced practical protective gear such as veils and

(Far right) Chanel's grey silk jersey chemise frock trimmed with grey rabbit fur and girdled with a length of grey jersey. Reproduced from American *Vogue*, 1 August 1917

By 1917 American *Vogue* had declared Chanel 'Dictator of Jersey' for she had successfully elevated the fabric from its humble status giving it equal rank with the other classic materials of the time, serge and *velours de laine*. This dress was a model she wore herself. *Vogue* said 'The war puts its ban on the bizarre in frocks; they must be safe and sane… unobtrusive…' or , like this one, 'correctly sober and expensively smart'.

Chanel's slip-over, American *Vogue*, 1 June 1917

This successful garment is here interpreted in emerald green silk jersey, equipped with useful pockets and is finished with green *coroso* (palm nut) buttons. It was developed from the *tricot marinière* first introduced at Deauville.

goggles and heavy, warm, waterproofed cloth coats to keep out the damp, dust and cold. For the wealthy, garments were custom-made by a couture house or a *modiste* or dressmaker, but ready-made clothing was beginning to be available and was sold by the large department stores as well as in some smaller dress shops and from mail-order catalogues.

The progressive Paris couturier Paul Poiret was a major fashion force from 1908. He pioneered a straighter, high-waisted line in a neo-classical revival style. One year later he incorporated this into his costumes inspired by the Orient, which coincided with the sensational success of Serge Diaghilev's Ballets Russes' first Paris season in 1909. The dancers wore dramatic eastern costumes and danced amidst exotic interiors designed by Léon Bakst. The Ballets Russes and Poiret's clothing introduced a riot of bold colours into fashion. Poiret dressed his daring customers in rich brocaded textiles and harem pantaloons, wrapping their heads in exotic, plumed turbans and covering their wrists and ankles with bangles. Poiret boasted that he released women from the bonds of the tight-waisted corset because his straight garments required only a smooth and straight elasticated undergarment. However, around 1910, he restrained them again in hobble skirts.

This was the background against which Chanel introduced her relaxed jersey sports suits at the beginning of the First World War.

Recent reproduction of jersey suit made by the House of Chanel after an illustration of Chanel's jersey suits in *Les Elégances Parisiennes*, May 1916.

Chanel showed her first complete couture collection in the Autumn of 1916 following the opening of her Biarritz house. 'Women are claiming the masculine advantage of pockets', reported *Vogue* in the same year. The war outlawed extravagance and Chanel capitalised on this, providing women with versatile clothing in practical colours.

Les Dernières Créations de la Mode, from *Les Elégances Parisiennes*, March 1917.

Three years into the war, coal and oil were in short supply but it was still possible for fashion magazines to discuss the latest materials available from the textile manufacturers. This illustration heads a description of a range of products from flowered silk foulards, satins and taffetas to linens, supple wools and printed crepes. Chanel combined jersey from the firms of Rodier with plaids in outfits like the one second from the right.

DEAUVILLE

On the eve of the First World War Deauville was an internationally renowned resort on Normandy's *Côte Fleurie*, with a substantial population during the high season. It was fashionable, a summer playground for aristocrats and the *nouveaux riches* who entertained themselves with promenading, sailing, boating, racing, polo and the casino.

In the summer of 1913, Boy Capel took a suite at the Normandy Hotel, and arranged for Chanel to open a shop in the smartest street in the town, the rue Gontaut-Biron. The shop, its striped awning clearly announcing the name of Chanel in capital letters, was located between the Normandy Hotel, the casino and the beach. Bathing at this time was not yet practised by all, and bathing dresses were cumbersome and all-enveloping. Porcelain-pale complexions were protected from the sun by large hats and parasols.

Chanel, who adored the beach, sea-bathing and relaxing in the sun, had anticipated the growing popularity of sportswear and the need for practical but elegant styles for relaxing and outdoor living. Deauville was the ideal spot to market her own particular taste in clothing for the kind of lifestyle with which she herself was now familiar.

Among Chanel's first clients at Deauville was Antoinette Bernstein, the wife of playwright Henri Bernstein, who was to become a close friend. The Bernsteins had already visited Chanel and Capel in their Paris apartment. Other clients soon followed. The Baroness Henri 'Kitty' de Rothschild, who abandoned Poiret in favour of Chanel, claimed to be an early promoter of the young dressmaker. Cécile Sorel, a leading actress of the Théâtre de Paris, was also dressed by Chanel.

It is difficult to say exactly when Chanel began selling sweaters and jersey garments as well as hats, and little is known of her workroom practices. Existing evidence often conflicts. Suzanne Orlandi may have been one of the first women to own a dress designed by Chanel in 1913. This was made of black velvet with a high waistline and was finished with a white petal collar – a dramatic combination which was to become one of Chanel's trademarks in later years. Some maintain that Chanel only sold a ready-to-wear range at Deauville, her first couture collection coming later.

Several anecdotes relate the origins of the Chanel sweater. Possibly the most convincing tells how Chanel picked up a polo player's sweater to wear because she felt cold. Having adjusted a belt over it and pushed up the sleeves to make it fit she decided that a similar garment in the right size could be very becoming and had some made to sell in the Deauville shop. They were an immediate success.

Whatever its origins, the loose-fitting sweater was adopted by many women during the First World War. By 1917, it was a general fashion with versions of the basic shape available in silk and wool. *Vogue,* in the issue of 1 June in that year, illustrates Chanel's 'slip-over sweater' (see page 13) of emerald green silk with green coroso buttons. In the same year advertisements for similar garments by manufacturers like James McCreery and Co., New York, appeared 'with popular large collars and cuffs'. British *Vogue* carried an advertisement for 'Elenid Jersey Connoisseur' of Bond Street, London in 1919. The basic style had changed very little, retaining the sailor collar and long, easy line and clearly filled an international need.

Chanel had an ally in the caricaturist Sem, who lampooned high fashion in his series *Le Vrai et le Faux Chic* (True and False Chic) which first appeared in *L'Illustration,* 28 March 1914. Sem criticised the bad taste and pomposity of *faux chic,* comparing foolish, ostentatious dress with the elegant lines of a Chanel suit worn by the *demi-mondaine* Forsane. Sem's work further promoted Chanel and shows us she was a readily identifiable society figure when he made the drawing of Boy as a polo-playing centaur, catching Coco the milliner in his arms (see page 6). This caricature was published in 1913.

On 3 August 1914, Germany formally declared war on France. Chanel's time had come. She flourished not just in spite of the war, but perhaps because of it. Against the background of war and rationing, good taste demanded that women finally pare down their clothing, rejecting conspicuous opulence and frou-frou. Women were also facing a need for practical clothing to suit a new, active lifestyle as they became involved in the war effort. Looking back on this period, Chanel once said she had believed that the Germans were going to war to prevent her making hats!

The following day, Britain entered the war, and by the end of the month Boy had left Deauville. Deauville rapidly emptied as the French government gave the order to mobilise troops, but Chanel did not close the shop. Some of the women who remained did voluntary work at the hospital and it has been suggested that Chanel herself took up nursing, allowing the back room of her shop to be used for meetings and shrewdly creating elegant nursing outfits for wealthy volunteers.

Events moved swiftly: the Germans reached Saint-Quentin on 27 August and Paris was effectively cut off. In September the French government moved to Bordeaux. Now many wealthy people fled to Deauville, and Chanel's boutique, the only one left open in the town, offered them chic, practical sports clothing equally suitable for the golf course or war relief work.

At the beginning of the war, a narrow silhouette was fashionable. Shorter, fuller skirts were gradually adopted for ease of movement for the various activities women now found themselves engaged in. Many society women donned the uniform of the Red Cross, and at the very least would help to raise money for this organisation, or knit comforts for soldiers. Others took to driving army cars and ambulances, factory work or farm labouring.

Many of these jobs were hard, dirty and sometimes dangerous. Women wore protective clothing in the form of serge suits and cotton overalls or dungarees. Trousers were worn for many occupations, and outerwear, such as heavy woollen

Chanel's coat of tartan and jersey, American *Vogue,* 15 February 1917.

The *jupe tonneau* or barrel skirt launched by the French couturiers was more successful in the USA than in a Paris restrained by the sorrows of war. *Vogue* announced 'Barrel outlines and normal waistlines are signs of Spring in Paris' and went on to praise this coat of grey *chanella,* a fine, textured jersey, faced with red and green tartan with a pleated tartan overskirt. The outfit is shown with a hat by Reboux. These models were imported into the United States by J.M. Gidding – wealthy American socialites were still eager for news of Paris fashions in spite of the fact that imports to the USA had been halved. To counter copyists, the *Chambre Syndicale de la Couture Parisienne* ruled out publication of magazine coverage of their designs until after the collections had been shown in February and August each year.

Embroidered satin dress
by Chanel, American *Vogue*
15 March 1917

This black satin dress
was exotically embroidered 'to
the limit' in white, green, grey
and yellow silks. The tunic
effect is a softened version
of the barrel line.

overcoats and rubberised cloth trenchcoats, was introduced into women's wardrobes.
As yet, however, such garments were considered as workwear and uniforms, not
fashion, and magazines like British *Vogue*, launched in 1916, barely devoted space to
them, balancing articles on how to dress on a reduced income during wartime with
reports of the latest Paris fashions.

In Europe the war enforced sobriety, paving the way for changes in dress to which
Chanel was a major contributor. Her smart, modern look had become a great success
and she now had more clients than ever.

Once the crisis diminished, people began to return to Paris. Chanel herself also
returned, leaving others to run her Deauville shop.

257　　　　　258　　　　　259

COSTUMES DE JERSEY
Modèles de Gabrielle Chanel (fig. 257, 258 et 259)

'Costumes de Jersey' from
Les Elégances Parisiennes,
March 1917

These three model suits by
Chanel repeat the use of
simple, open-necked blouses
with sailor collars worn
underneath comfortable
loosely-belted slip-overs and
the new, fuller, shorter skirts.
Ease and luxury are combined
in the marriage of fluid jersey
with detailed silk embroidery
in the models at left and
centre, while the sensible
beige costume on the right has
a double-buckled belt derived
from saddlery. Chic plain
accessories complete the
uncluttered Chanel look.
Interestingly, the central figure
is wearing two-tone shoes,
here in beige and blue, a
classic Chanel theme which
remains popular today (see
page 112).

BIARRITZ

As the war progressed, magazines reported that Paris was becoming dull. People in search of a more joyful atmosphere were leaving for neutral Spain, the Riviera and Biarritz. Those who stayed in Paris participated in the war effort by organising and contributing to charity fêtes.

Biarritz, a fashionable, cosmopolitan resort on the Bay of Biscay in south-west France, catered for the idle rich who retreated there from the reminders of war. Society had first followed the Empress Eugénie and her court to Biarritz in the 19th century, and it had not lost any of its allure.

In 1915 Boy Capel was transferred from the army to the wartime Franco-British Commission, aided in this by his friendship with Georges Clemenceau, who later became France's Prime Minister. Free at last to return to France, Boy chose to visit Biarritz with Chanel. Both of them realised that the wealthy refugees wanted luxury in their lives, and set out to exploit the business potential of the resort, as they had at Deauville. However, Chanel did not restrict herself to a boutique selling hats and sports clothes; she opened a *maison de couture* as well. Her first fashion house in Biarritz opened in July 1915 in a villa facing the casino on the rue Gardères. Once again, Capel raised the capital. The business was so successful that Chanel was later able to reimburse him the full 300,000 francs. (The Biarritz house eventually closed in 1927, having firmly established Chanel as a leading couturière.)

The Biarritz couture house was staffed by Chanel's younger sister Antoinette, and some of the employees from the rue Cambon. Local help was hired to swell the staff to some 60 workers. Chanel had learned the importance of setting up a workroom staffed by skilled specialists. Mme Marie-Louise Deray began as a manager of Chanel's Biarritz workroom in 1915, and was later to move to the Paris headquarters, becoming one of the mainstays of the firm. The clientèle included wealthy socialites as well as actresses and singers who were often Chanel's friends, such as the opera singer Martha Davelli. Some of the most important customers came from nearby Spain including members of the Spanish royal family and aristocracy. According to Mme Deray, Chanel 'sold a great deal to Spain – San Sebastian, Bilbao – wherever there were elegant women and money'. (Pierre Galante, p.37)

Chanel's methods of working are also described: she was irascible and autocratic. Apparently, she did not enter the workrooms herself, but after she had chosen the materials, would gather her staff together to explain to them what she wanted. She needed to prove her authority but at the same time often failed to find the correct terms in which to express her requirements to her staff. When the desired results were not produced, unpleasant scenes ensued. Chanel may have learned to sew at the convent, but she was often criticised for her lack of technical knowledge. In spite of this, she had innate flair, creating lovely garments in jerseys and cottons. Deray claimed that Chanel was helped by industrialists from Tours in the Loire valley. She chose everything herself; silks, wools, lace, ornaments and colours were selected from the best that the Lyon and Scottish dyers could provide. In spite of the war a trade in luxury textiles continued.

Chanel's methods were a test of endurance for her mannequins who had to stand for an exhausting six to seven hours while Chanel fitted the models. She is said to have insisted on up to 30 fittings of a toile or muslin pattern. She did not produce designs on paper, preferring instead to work like an *essayeuse* or fitter in the tailoring tradition using pins to drape and fit the garment on the body. Mme Deray also stated that Chanel paid her mannequins 100 francs a month. In 1918 this represented a tiny proportion of the cost of one of her dresses, yet she refused to raise their salaries: 'They're beautiful girls. Let them take lovers'.

Arriving in her chauffeur-driven Rolls-Royce at midday, Chanel would stay until 2 or 3 o'clock, according to the importance of her customers. She would then retire to

Four illustrations of Chanel
garments, American *Vogue*,
1 November 1918

Fur trimming continued to
feature prominently in Chanel's
winter collections for both
indoor and outdoor wear.

This page: Black satin frock
decorated with white angora
and black beads.

Facing page: (Left) Black tulle
gown edged with *ziblinette* and
wood-coloured beads. (Centre)
Brown *charmeuse* costume
trimmed with castor. (Right)
Brown velvet coat with deep
bands and scarf collar of
peruvienne fur.

her private drawing-room where she would entertain. Quite clearly, she put a great
deal more work into building up the House than this writer implies. However, views
like this contribute to building up an image of herself as a person of leisure that
Chanel had been carefully constructing from early in her career.

Already, in 1915, *Harper's Bazaar* could proclaim that 'The woman who hasn't at
least one Chanel is hopelessly out of the running in fashion'. In 1916 the same
American publication reproduced a drawing of Chanel's embroidered chemise dress,
as made at the Biarritz House.

By this date the American market formed a major part of Chanel's clientèle. *Vogue*
sighted her jersey dresses at Palm Beach, Florida, in April 1917. Chanel was already
designing loose-fitting styles with sashes or belts draped easily around the hips. By
1917 *Harper's* could confidently state that 'This season the name of Gabrielle Chanel
is on the lips of every buyer'. With Antoinette in charge at Biarritz, Chanel was able
to move confidently between the bases of her empire. By 1916 the combined staff of
Paris, Deauville and Biarritz totalled 300.

Evening dress by Chanel, 1919 (Details of bodice and skirt)

Silk chiffon tabard style dress decorated with glass beads and gelatin *pailletes* in a design of circular motifs and abstracted foliate imagery. It was worn by the Hon Mrs Anthony Henley at celebrations associated with the Peace Conference in 1919 and is the earliest Chanel garment in the V&A Collection.

Victoria & Albert Museum, London (T.85 & A-1974)

Everything Chanel did made news, including the sun tan which she cultivated. Up until this time tanned skin had been associated with the labouring classes. Suddenly sun bathing was *de rigueur*.

From 1917, designers began to introduce the barrel skirt, which at its most extreme tapered towards the hem from exaggeratedly wide hips. Chanel followed this line to a certain extent but also showed slimmer, slightly flared skirts, often softly pleated. By 1919, Chanel's much slimmer silhouette had a mid-calf-length skirt and a lower, looser waistline.

Besides jersey, Chanel made much use of other materials, including suede for hats, belts and jackets. For example, a white suede coat was lined throughout with cerise jersey cloth and was worn over a frock of the same fabric. This practice of matching the lining of a coat or jacket to the dress or blouse beneath was still common in Chanel's suits of the 1950s and 1960s. Check-patterned cloths were another favourite for sports suits. Although many daytime models were created in jersey, Chanel also chose to use satin, tulle and velvet for afternoon and evening dresses.

The typical wartime Paris frock in sombre grey did not appeal to the American market, for which Chanel produced outfits such as one in green cloth with bright red and green embroidery in her 1917 collections. Her favourite colours at this time

were reds, such as Bordeaux, embroidered in gold and dull-coloured silks. Deep blue, *marron* and other dark grounds as well as black might be embroidered in colourful barbaric or oriental motifs.

Chanel loved furs; *Vogue* frivolously reported that the shortage of coal had increased the Parisienne's demand for fur garments, although these too were in short supply. In 1917, Chanel showed a taupe velvet wrap edged with bands of beaver. In the following year, furs of 'indefinite extraction', such as *peruvienne* and *ziblinette* were used to trim coats and even evening dresses; one stunning example of black tulle was also embellished with beads. Rabbit and squirrel also featured, while white angora edged a black satin dress with bead embroidery.

Before the end of the war some younger women had begun to reduce their wardrobes and no longer made the once obligatory change into afternoon gowns but in Europe black continued to be worn extensively. In April 1919, American *Vogue* covered Chanel's collections in a lengthy article praising the understanding of modern post-war life which she reflected in her models. 'Mlle Chanel has confined herself almost entirely to black costumes for evening wear, and these costumes are short and round of corsage, so that they might even be worn in the afternoon under a long *manteau*.'

In 1919, Chanel showed evening dresses without sleeves, often in tulle with uneven hemlines and floating drapery, decorated with jet or ostrich feathers. Many of her evening *manteaux* had collars made like crossed scarves. And Chanel's dignified georgette crepe gown for the woman of middle age appearing in the same year was discreetly described as 'reticent as to the exact lines of the legs'.

Chanel's sister Antoinette married in 1919 and it is believed that Chanel designed her wedding gown. A Chanel wedding dress is illustrated in the American *Vogue* of Spring 1919, but, unfortunately, there is no evidence that this was the model for Antoinette. One month later, the same magazine was reporting on Chanel's new 'engaging' rubber raincoats 'always practical, easy to wear and fastening close and high at the neck' and made in white, rose, blue and black on the lines of a coachman's or chauffeur's coat. A feature of these coats were the scarf ends incorporated into the collar, a feature which Chanel was to use again.

Also in this year Chanel returned to the theatre to dress Vera Sergine for a new play by her friend Henri Bernstein.

CHANEL'S USE OF JERSEY FABRICS

During the 19th century, outdoor garments made from knitted materials were considered smart for the first time and the jersey costume appeared about 1879. Made of a finely-knitted silk or wool, it clung to the figure, creating a close-fitting sheath-like form. Heavier, knitted sweaters were also worn with a flannel or linen skirt for tennis and golf, and it was also used for children's sports and beach wear. Fine, silk stockinettes had long been used for gloves and hosiery, and woollen jersey was particularly associated with men's natural-coloured underwear.

Chanel made knitted jersey a high-fashion material. Although she was not the only couturière to use this fabric, she was considered its greatest exponent, and by 1917 her business earned from *Vogue* the title of 'The Jersey House'. Jersey not only overtook twill-woven serge as the fabric for dresses and ensembles of the war years, but remained in favour long afterwards, and has always been seen in Chanel collections. Jersey retains its popularity today, with an abundance of these knitted fabrics available in synthetic as well as natural fibres.

In 1916 Chanel purchased an unsold stock of jersey from the firm of Jean Rodier. It had been intended to make sports clothes for men. The stretchy nature of jersey made it a challenge to work with but Chanel succeeded in overcoming the problems by making simple, supple shapes.

The results were sensational studies in simplicity and chic, so different from the extravaganzas of Paul Poiret. During the war Chanel wore the large jersey coats herself. These are illustrated in the issue of British *Vogue*, 1 October 1917. Each has a deep collar and a full, short skirt – shorter than the dress beneath. As well as jersey, velvet and satin were used in these coats, all trimmed with rabbit fur. Fur was also used to adorn jersey dresses, particularly the hemlines.

The magazine *Les Elégances Parisiennes* acclaimed Chanel's jersey designs in the issue of 15 March 1917. Using Chanel garments to illustrate the article it mentions jersey in the same sentence as cashmere and describes Rodier's latest *djersabure*, a thick and rough fabric with large stitches, which draped beautifully into soft pleats.

By now Chanel was well known on both sides of the Atlantic. In its issue of 17 March 1917 American *Vogue* reported on her use of Rodier's new beige *djersabure* fabric for her sports coats. Despite the feeling that jersey was 'no longer smart, we persist in wearing it, and like good people, the couturiers continue to supply us with frocks of this comfortable, satisfactory stuff'. The 15 September 1917 report is more enthusiastic, reproducing samples of Rodier fabrics such as *djersagolf*, a black and white plaid for sportswear.

Jersey replaced familiar materials like serge because of shortages during the First World War which made them scarce and expensive. Serge was in demand for

Left, Wedding gown by Chanel, American *Vogue*, Spring 1919

A short white satin wedding gown swathed with a white mantle of Chantilly lace and overdress of the same fabric. The dress, with its low waistline and drapery falling into points, anticipates the styles of the 1920s.

Right, Black lace gown by Chanel, American *Vogue*, Spring 1919

This delicate and fragile gown of black Chantilly lace layered over a bodice of gold net is trimmed with jet beading around the waist and the beaded side-panels on the skirt end in jet tassels at the hem. Fringes and tassels feature regularly in Chanel's work. For example, she made a fringed skirt for a coat dress accessorised by a neckerchief inspired by the American Westerns seen at the cinema. *Vogue* acclaimed this *nonchalance de luxe* as 'the sort of simplicity that always has been and always will be expensive'.

uniforms for the armed forces. Like serge, jersey was cool and light, and available in many colours. It could be embroidered, trimmed with other cloths, elaborate braids, fur or leather, and varied in weight depending on whether it was made of a light silk or heavy wool. In 1917 *Vogue* reported that all the great couture houses were making use of silk or wool jersey for their tailored frocks, afternoon gowns and *manteaux*, and sang its praises beneath the headline 'jersey defies passing fashion'. It was already accepted as a classic by this time.

Chanel was to continue to feature jersey in her collections for its comfort and drape. Between 1915 and 1920 it was used in a whole range of garments, from the long-line sweaters and jackets with capacious pockets, plain sports suits and severe capes of beige jersey, to dresses combining silk jersey and lace. On 15 March 1917 American *Vogue* commented: 'One of the newest whims of Chanel is the combination of silk and wool jersey. Some of the newest models are quite untrimmed save for such varying textures as appears in this frock of Bordeaux wool jersey, liberally trimmed in deep bands and yoke with silk jersey of the same colour.' Chanel chose a limited variety of colours from beige, sand, grey and black to blue, green, cerise and red. The beige might be set off by trimming or embroidery in blue, grey by red , and blue by brown or gold. A costume of blue jersey had a belt and collar of brown suede embroidered with blue silk. Chanel frequently edged her jersey costumes with fur, such as the grey rabbit on a grey silk jersey dress of 1917, and monkey fur on a black silk jersey coat for Cécile Sorel.

A fine-textured jersey known as *chanella* is mentioned in American *Vogue* in their issue of 15 February 1917. The name suggests that this *chanella* may have been manufactured specially for Chanel by Rodier. The illustration which accompanies the report teams grey *chanella* with bright red and green tartan

PARIS

Many of Chanel's biographers give the impression that she became a couturière by chance or whim, whereas in fact she had strong business sense and the backing of an intelligent, influential partner in Boy Capel. She learned her business through experience, and it is often said that her genius lay in her ability to absorb details, if not the necessary skills to accomplish them herself – she soon came to know who could provide these skills and how to get the best out of them for her own purposes. She exploited everything available to her – the war shortages which may have led her to invest in jersey, her celebrated, rich and influential friends, even the very circumstances of the war itself which drew society to the resorts of Deauville and Biarritz. Paris in wartime may have been 'dull', but society flocked to Chanel. Women ordered dresses by the dozen.

Chanel was shrewd. Having gained status as a fashionable couturière, she herself also became a celebrity. Her social circle extended to include writers and artists. She already had many theatrical friends, and in 1913 had herself become a pupil of the dancer Caryathis, accompanying her to the première of the Ballets Russes' *Le Sacre du Printemps* (The Rite of Spring) in May 1913. At the beginning of the century, when short-haired women were considered bizarre and scandalous, the avant-garde Caryathis had dispensed with long tresses, and the writer Colette had also sacrificed her long plaits. Six years later, in 1908, Poiret made his models cut their hair. In 1917 Chanel followed suit. And she set a trend for women the world over. The Chanel legend cites an accident with a water-heater as the reason. Determined to attend the Opera, she cut off her hair to disguise the damage. In September 1919 Henri Bernstein introduced Chanel to his friend Liane de Pougy, who described her as looking like a little street urchin with her short hair-style and thin, wiry physique.

Chanel was introduced to Misia Sert in 1917 at a dinner party given by Cécile Sorel. Misia was to become Chanel's only true woman friend and one of the most important figures in her life – acknowledged tutor in cultural and aesthetic matters.

In 1914 Misia had married the fashionable artist José Maria Sert, becoming involved through him with Diaghilev and the artists of the Ballets Russes. Misia herself, on her first meeting with Chanel, was struck by her generosity and grace; as the two women were saying goodnight, Misia admired Chanel's ravishing fur-trimmed, red velvet coat, which Chanel at once took off and placed on Misia's shoulders, saying that she would be happy to give it to her.

With success there were also sorrows. As she gained wealth and independence she and Boy Capel began to drift apart, and she finally realised that he would never offer to marry her. Instead in October 1918 he married Lady Diana Wyndham. Lady Diana had already lost both her brother and her first husband in the war and then, tragically, Boy was killed in a motoring accident as he travelled from Paris to Cannes on Christmas Eve, 1919. Chanel was devastated. Boy had continued to visit her at her rented villa in Saint-Cloud even after his marriage. An old friend, Léon de Laborde, broke the news and Chanel immediately set out with him for Cannes, but arrived too late for the funeral. Years later, she would say that when she lost Boy, she lost everything.

In spite of the tragedy Chanel's business continued to thrive and she later described 1919 as the year 'I woke up famous'.

Two THE 1920s

Throughout the 1920s Paris continued to dominate international fashion and the couture trades enjoyed boom years. The leading fashion houses included Chanel, Patou, Vionnet, Lanvin, Callot Soeurs, Cheruit and by the late 1920s also included the talents of Elsa Schiaparelli. Fashion in the 1920s evolved towards what became known as the Garçonne Look and it was Chanel and her great rival Jean Patou who became the best known exponents of this style.

Deauville and Biarritz remained fashionable seaside resorts in the post-war years and Chanel's boutiques continued to enjoy good business. Cannes became another exclusive resort and Chanel opened another branch there. During the early 1920s Chanel's workrooms, opened in 1919 at 25 rue Cambon, expanded to include numbers 27, 29 and 31, where she was officially registered as a couturière and where the House still rents the premises today. In about 1928 she installed faceted glass mirrors into her couture salon to create a Modernist impression of endless space. Indeed, the minimalism of her professional interior was to reflect and reinforce her clothing aesthetic. In complete contrast, Chanel's private salon on the third floor of number 31 was lavishly decorated: she believed that clutter was acceptable in a room, but unnecessary in clothes. Louis XIV furniture was freely combined with 18th-century Venetian mirrors and blackamoors, lacquered Coromandel screens, elegant smoked crystal and amethyst chandeliers and exotic artefacts from the east, including several pairs of carved wooden animals. Lions, in honour of her birth sign, were Chanel's particular favourite. The walls were covered with gold-painted stretched silk, the carpets were beige and the upholstery was of matching suede. Chanel loved white flowers which she displayed in abundance, particularly her favourite white lilies. It was here that she received her friends and most-favoured clients.

During the 1920s Chanel was patronised by a prestigious international clientèle which included Baroness de Rothschild, Countess Anne de Noailles, the Duchess of York (later Queen Elizabeth, mother of the present Queen of England), the Duchess of Beaufort, Daisy Fellowes, Baba d'Erlanger, Paula Gellibrand, the Ranee of Pudakota and Princess Marthe Bibesco. Some clients, including Princess Bibesco, modelled her clothes for society and fashion magazines which gave the House name additional kudos. British actress Gertrude Lawrence was also a client and so was Hollywood star Ina Claire. The latter wore Chanel's clothes on and off the screen and was photographed wearing Chanel by Edward Steichen for American *Vogue* in 1925. Most couture clients paid on account, some monthly and others annually.

By the 1920s Chanel was actively involved in the design and making of her

clothes but kept herself remote and impersonal in business transactions. She rarely dealt directly with clients, recognising that her role was to create mystique and herself epitomise her design philosophy. She reinforced her personification of the House style by generally using dark-haired models, whose looks resembled her own. From 1925 she employed her society friend Sarah Arkwright, popularly known as Vera Bate, to wear her clothes at all times and, when asked, to reveal the name of her couturière.

Chanel bought a large ground-floor flat in the Hôtel de Lauzan, an 18th-century mansion at 29 rue du Faubourg Saint Honoré, where her neighbours were the Rothschilds and the President of France. She also regularly stayed in her private suite at the Ritz Hotel, conveniently located just behind the rue Cambon in the Place Vendôme. In the 1920s Chanel was described as starting work at noon and then continuing until seven or eight o'clock in the evening. In a letter to his wife, Clementine, written in 1927 Winston Churchill described his impression of Chanel and the frantic pace of her life:

'She hunted vigorously all day, motored to Paris after dinner, and is today engaged in passing and improving dresses on endless streams of mannequins. Altogether almost 200 models have to be settled in almost 3 weeks. Some have to be altered 10 times. She does it with her own fingers, pinning, cutting, looping etc...'
(Leslie Field, p.201)

Interior of Chanel's flat

Chanel's private apartment is situated above the couture house at 31 rue Cambon and today is carefully preserved as a shrine to the founder. This room features one of her beloved lacquered Coromandel screens, and chairs upholstered with suede. Chanel liked clothes that were understated but thought that decoration in abundance was acceptable in the home.

Chanel was known to be a hard taskmaster, often making her house models stand deathly still while she pinned and tucked a garment until she was fully satisfied that it combined elegance with ease of movement. She rarely sketched her designs onto paper, preferring to work with the fabric directly on the body. First a muslin toile – a blueprint of the finished garment – would be made, and then, when this was perfect, it would be used as a pattern for making the final version in the selected fabric and trimmings.

Sleeve detail of a Chanel coat, 1927

Chanel always paid special attention to the cut of her sleeves so that they would allow complete ease of movement, without distorting the line of the garment. This detail, with its three rows of angled pin tucking at the elbow, reveals one stylish solution.

Throughout her career, Chanel was particularly obsessed with the cut of sleeves, constantly seeking to create those which would allow the wearer to move her arms without distorting the line of the garment. During the 1930s Diana Vreeland, the influential editor of *Harper's Bazaar*, became friends with Chanel and regularly bought her clothes. She was one of the very few, privileged clients to be fitted in Chanel's private atelier and stated:

'Coco was a nut on armholes. She never, ever got an armhole quite, quite perfect, the way she wanted it. She was always snipping and taking out sleeves, driving the tailors crazy. She'd put pins in me so I'd be all contorted, and she'd be talking and talking and giving me all sorts of philosophical observations...'
(Diana Vreeland, p.127)

The structure of couture houses such as Chanel's was organised according to a rigid hierarchy. At the peak of the pyramid in the salon was the *Vendeuse*, the top sales person; she was assisted by sales assistants, who were often ex-models, and who were called *Habilleuses*. In the workrooms the *Première Main* was ultimately responsible for the finished product and directed the *Seconde* and the *Petite Main*, whose tasks included finishing the garments. The *Arpètes* were young apprentices who started their careers in fashion with the most menial tasks, such as picking up the pins and sweeping the floors. There were separate workrooms for tailoring and dressmaking, for the making of accessories and for decorative techniques such as beading and embroidery, although Chanel also sent work to external specialist workshops, such as Lesage. Chanel's own employees numbered between 2000 and 3000 during the 1920s, when business boomed.

FASHION 1920 TO 1924: CHANEL'S SLAV PERIOD

From 1920 to 1923 Chanel had a romantic affair with the Grand Duke Dmitri Pavlovitch, grandson of Czar Alexander II, and the two remained close friends thereafter. Chanel met Dmitri before the First World War and when he returned to Paris, this time impoverished, she supported him. As always, Chanel's personal life was to exert a profound influence upon her design work.

From 1920 to 1924 hemlines crept up from the ankle to around mid-calf level and waistlines gradually moved from their natural position down to the hips. The cut of women's clothes became increasingly straight and these solid blocks of fabric became ideal grounds for luxurious beaded and embroidered decoration.

During the late 19th century the Slav revival in Russia created renewed interest in traditional folk art. Colourful peasant embroideries and woodcuts influenced many Russian designers who were later to bring their enthusiasm to Paris. These included such notable figures as Erté, Sonia Delaunay and Léon Bakst, whose designs for the Ballets Russes had a profound influence upon fashion and interior design. During the early 1920s the fashion houses were starved of fine fabrics, following the interruption in production brought about by the war. On the whole the textiles that were available were plain and these were embellished with rich embroidered designs to provide luxurious couture fabrics.

In the years following the Revolution many exiled Russian aristocrats settled in Paris. Many of the women, who had previously embroidered as a leisure activity, now

THE PEASANT LOOK

used their skills to earn a living by opening machine- and hand-embroidery workshops to supply the couture houses.

Chanel's fashion collections drew extensively upon Russian influences during the early 1920s, but regrettably it appears that no items of dress have survived. However, fashion magazines of the period describe her loose shift dresses, tunics, crepe de chine blouses, waistcoats and evening coats made in dark or neutral colours and adorned with exquisite, vividly coloured embroidery in naive Russian peasant designs. These became so popular that in 1921 Chanel opened her own workshop, which was run by Dmitri's sister, the Grand Duchess Maria Pavlovna. In 1922 Chanel introduced a version of the roubachka, the long, belted blouse worn by Russian peasant women, but made in luxurious silk crepe de chine for her couture clientèle. Once again, the Orient also became a popular source of inspiration for interior and fashion designers during the early 1920s and some of Chanel's dresses, shawls and textiles were beaded or embroidered utilising Chinese decorative motifs. Maria soon opened her own workshop, called Kitmir, and from the start, had an assured client in Chanel, until she built up her business and started also to work for other couturiers.

By 1923 Chanel further simplified the design and decoration of her fashions. There was less use of brocades and fewer embroidered garments in each collection, although these items became popular staple lines. In that year Chanel's favourite colour combination for embroideries was beige and red, executed in geometric designs on a black or brown ground. This reflected general trends in design which were witnessing a move away from the exuberance of Art Deco in favour of the more austere, crisp lines of Modernism. Brown and beige were particularly favourite House colours while grey, dark green, navy blue, white and black were regularly used. Deep burgundy reds to palest rose petal pink were much used for evening gowns.

During the 1920s the major fabrics which appeared in Chanel's collections were silk crepe de chine, georgette, chiffon, velvet, kasha, wool tweed and jersey textiles.

Illustration of Chanel's roubachka (left) and embroidered dress (right), 1922

Long belted blouse in black crepe de chine with square neckline and embroidered with naive Russian designs. Reproduced from *Vogue* 1922. Chanel was particularly noted for her beautiful embroidered clothes during the early 1920s. This garment, inspired by the roubachka worn by muzhik – Russian peasants – is teamed with a long, lean skirt.

Detail of beaded and
embroidered silk evening
dress worn by the Hon. Mrs
Anthony Henley, 1922. See
also page 34

A close-up of the work
produced by Chanel's
embroidery workshops during
the early 1920s. The tension
of this embroidered and
beaded decoration has
decoratively puckered the
silk ground to create an
interesting surface texture.
The rounded motifs applied to
this dress are characteristic of
Art Deco design at this date.

Victoria & Albert Museum,
London (T.86-1974)

Chanel's beaded and embroidered silk evening dress worn by the Hon. Mrs Anthony Henley, 1922

The design of this sleeveless dress, which flares from the hips to an uneven hemline, is typical of the early 1920s. The straight tabard panels are embellished with clear glass bugle beads and gold metallic and black thread embroidery, applied in circular motifs and loops. This disc decoration is carried onto the silk inserts that trail from the hips below the hem of the tabard. These have three silk half-circles applied each side. There is a black silk chemise with a machine-lace edged hem.

Victoria & Albert Museum, London (T.86-1974)

Red silk evening dress by Chanel, early 1920s

Chanel loved bright red and regularly used it for day and evening wear. This evening dress with two gathered tiers allowed ease of movement for the wearer to walk and dance while creating the fashionable lean line. Its solid colour is broken by the diagonal rows of pin tucking and two decorative clusters of fabric.

Chanel's evening shoes, early 1920s

These open-sided, T-bar, shoes of red silk with gold piping and heels studded with diamanté decoration were designed to be worn with Chanel's red dress illustrated above. Decorative shoes like these were very popular for dancing during the 1920s.

In spite of the availability of more traditional couture fabrics, Chanel continued to use great quantities of jersey, the natural pliancy of which was ideally suited to her comfortable, understated cardigan suits. Many of Chanel's wool and cotton jersey fabrics were enriched with silk to provide light weight, warmth and lustre for added luxury. So great was demand for this fabric, that Chanel opened her own factory in Asnières called Tricots Chanel. This meant she could control her own production and ensure design exclusivity. From 1928 to the end of 1933 Chanel employed the Russian Futurist poet Iliazd, who had previously worked with the artist Sonia Delaunay, to design textiles. He was initially employed as a draughtsman but from 1931 was appointed factory director, with special responsibility for the colouring and textures of Chanel's jerseys. By the late 1920s Chanel had started to work with other fabrics, including printing her own silks, and the factory name was changed to Tissus Chanel.

For the day time, Chanel used much Fair Isle and striped jersey, which she cut into cardigan suits and sweaters, often worn with plain pleated skirts. As always, the fashion press praised the ease, style and practicality of Chanel's clothes and marvelled at their versatility, which enabled clients to wear them throughout the day.

During the early 1920s Chanel introduced ensembles consisting of coats made from light wool or silk crepe, lined with foulard or printed crepe which matched the fabric of the dress worn underneath. This was a theme she was to continue to develop throughout her career.

In 1923 Chanel introduced cape sleeves, which she continued to use throughout the 1930s. The loose cut of cape sleeves combined ease of movement and elegance, the components so central to Chanel's work. Some of her coats had detachable fur capes. Chanel used fur to trim her garments regardless of the season and in 1923 she held a show in Deauville with Russian models displaying her range of furs.

By 1923 there was much debate about the future direction of the hemline and great variations existed from one couture house to another. Lengths ranged from ankle to mid-calf, as some predicted the hemline would lengthen and others anticipated that it would rise. Chanel, confident of future developments, made all of her garments with short skirts. She also designed dresses with concealed fullness to give an impression of the lean silhouette which anticipated future trends. Indeed, by 1923 Chanel had firmly laid the foundation for the Garçonne Look which dominated women's fashion from 1925 to 1929.

PERFUME

As one of the top fashion talents in Paris, Chanel was in a position to diversify into newly challenging and lucrative spin-off trades.

In 1921 she launched her first perfume, Chanel No. 5, reputedly her lucky number. No. 5 was a mixture of over 80 ingredients blended by the eminent French chemist, Ernest Beaux, who owned a laboratory in Grasse. It is believed that Dmitri introduced Chanel to Beaux, who was the chemist son of a former employee of the Czar's court. Beaux was at the forefront of the development of synthetic perfumes, using aldehydes to enhance the fragrance of costly natural ingredients such as jasmine, which is the base of No. 5.

Chanel designed the pharmaceutical, Modernist style bottle for No. 5 herself. Chanel No. 5 was the first perfume to bear a couturier's name on the label. Both this and the simple name of her fragrance were a far cry from the exotic names and decorative flacons which had characterised perfume in the pre-war years. Poiret was the first couturier to recognise that the sale of perfume was a successful adjunct to fashion sales, but his heady scents, named after his daughters, were based on natural sources and were never developed on such a large commercial scale.

Chanel, as ever, was shrewd in the launch of her new scent. Madsen states that

Chanel evening dress, 1923-4

Tabard style dress of tulle over silk, embroidered with silver bugle beads and pearl sequins. This dress was exhibited at the 1925 *L'Exposition des Arts Decoratifs et Industriels Modernes* in Paris at the *Palais des Elégances*. It has the couture number 10660.

Chanel knew the way to launch a luxury product was to make socialites think that they shared a responsibility for its success. He describes how Chanel returned to Paris with samples of Chanel No. 5, some of which she atomised in her fitting rooms. When her friends and clients asked if they could purchase it she claimed she had just had a small amount made for gifts, but if they thought it would sell she would market it.

No. 5 was sold from Chanel's shops in rue Cambon and at her boutiques in Deauville, Biarritz and Cannes. Cuir de Russie (1924), Bois des Iles (1926) and Gardenia (1927) were added to her fragrance range but, although successful, they never attained the lucrative sales of No. 5. In 1923, in a bid to widen the market for No. 5, Chanel asked Theophile Bader, owner of Galeries Lafayette, to retail it. He was interested but said that he would require greater quantities than Beaux could produce and suggested that he introduce her to Pierre and Paul Wertheimer, owners

Poster by Sem (George Goursat) advertising Chanel No. 5, 1920s

This poster, called *Le Nouveau Monde*, illustrates Chanel supervising a fitting, with bales of cloth at her side and framed within the confines of her perfume bottle. Sem's illustration reinforces how Chanel perfume and fashions were promoted to be inextricably entwined.

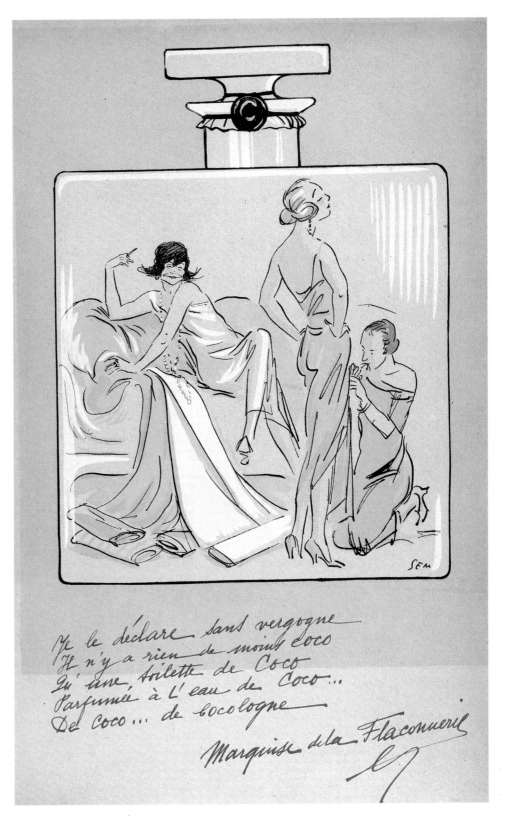

Detail of evening dress 1923-4

This detail shows the medieval-style scrollwork and heraldic motifs beaded onto the tabard of this dress and reveals the exquisite workmanship executed by Chanel's embroidery workrooms.

of one of France's largest cosmetic and fragrance companies, Les Parfumeries Bourjois. Chanel wanted to focus upon the fashion side of her business and agreed to let the Wertheimers produce and distribute her perfumes in return for which she would receive ten per cent of the profits.

Eventually her entire business would be owned by the Wertheimers, who continue to head the House of Chanel to the present day. Her perfumes were so successful and profitable that her royalties from their sales ensured Chanel financial independence for the rest of her life.

FASHION 1925 TO 1929 : THE GARÇONNE LOOK

From the end of the First World War, women's fashion evolved towards what became known in France as the Garçonne Look, which reached its peak in 1925 and continued with little change until 1929. This name was taken from Victor Margueritte's scandalous novel, *La Garçonne*, which was published in 1922, and told the story of a young woman who left the family home to make an independent life for herself. In Britain and America young women who adopted the new fashions were described as Flappers. In stark contrast to the mature, shapely ideal of the Edwardian period, fashion in the 1920s glorified the slender physique and was aimed at the younger woman. The ideal Garçonne woman had an androgynous figure and if this did not come naturally, the most determined followed a strict slimming régime. Clothes hung from the hips and shoulders and any hint of waist and bust was suppressed with straight elastic corsets. Dress lengths were gradually shortened to reach just below the knees when standing and to reveal them when seated – never before had women shown so much of their legs. Allowing ease of movement and comfort, this style of dress reflected women's increased emancipation in the post-war years.

Fashions in hairstyles also followed this trend towards the masculine and child-like, which characterised the Garçonne Look. By the 1920s a short hair style was essential to successfully sport the ubiquitous bell-shaped cloche hat which became an essential component of the Look. It was worn close to the head and pulled down deep over the brow. During the early 1920s fashion-conscious women bobbed or shingled their hair and by 1926 the most daring had it Eton-cropped, like that of a schoolboy. Chanel's Garçonne Look was also greatly inspired by the simplicity of design of men's everyday and sporting apparel, especially that worn by the fashionable Duke of Westminster and his circle.

Chanel was introduced to the Duke of Westminster, reported to be the wealthiest

Chanel's perfume packaging, 1920s

Chanel's first perfume, blended by Ernest Beaux, was launched in 1921. In stark contrast to the decorative flacons and exotic names given to perfumes in the pre-war years, Chanel gave her own name and a number, reputedly her lucky number, to the perfume. She designed the rather simple, pharmaceutical-style bottle and monochrome packaging herself.

Chanel wearing a Fair Isle cardigan, 1926

The original press caption for this photograph reads, 'Mme. Gabrielle Chanel, France's most famous woman dress-maker, who has become engaged to a British nobleman.' Chanel was much inspired by the clothes worn by the Duke of Westminster and his aristocratic friends, as well as those worn by working men. Following her fishing trips to Scotland with the duke, Chanel introduced tweeds and Fair Isle designs into her fashion collections.

man in England, in 1923 while on holiday in Monte Carlo with Vera Bate. The next day the duke invited the two friends to dine with him aboard his luxurious 40-cabin yacht, *The Flying Cloud*. The duke had recently become estranged from his wife, Violet Mary, Duchess of Westminster, and he soon fell under the spell of Chanel. Rumours of marriage subsequently appeared in the national press, but Chanel had no intention of giving up her business.

For the next seven years the duke, nicknamed 'Bendor' after his race horse which won the Derby, made frequent trips to Paris. Although Chanel refused to be away from the House of Chanel for too long she made many sailing trips with the duke and regularly stayed with him in England, where they hunted, played tennis, golf and fished for salmon. The clothes that the duke and his friends wore subsequently exerted a profound influence upon Chanel's clothing designs.

This inspiration from menswear combined function, comfort and durability and had the added kudos of an aristocratic design source. Blazers, waistcoats, cardigans, shirts with cuff-links and her famous tweeds were all inspired by the duke and his circle. Chanel was introduced to tweed on her Scottish fishing trips with Bendor. To secure her an exclusive product he bought her a tweed mill in Scotland which created a soft, lightweight woven fabric for her blazers and suits.

Chanel's collections were also influenced by more humble items of menswear, such as the sailor suit, reefer jacket, beret, mechanics' dungarees and stonemasons' neckerchiefs which she adapted for women and introduced into the luxury world of couture. Although not many women wore trousers other than for beach wear during the inter-war years, Chanel broke the taboo by designing and herself wearing loose sailor-style trousers which ended above the ankle.

Chanel's versatile clothes became hugely popular and were much copied, appealing to the contemporary woman who wanted to look sporty, even if she did not participate in any form of physical exercise. Chanel produced her classic sports costumes in jerseys or tweeds and sometimes combined the two. In 1927 she designed a black wool jersey cardigan costume lined with black silk satin which was worn with a green silk marocain blouse trimmed with the same satin. The skirts of these suits had a slight flare to facilitate movement and were sometimes pleated. Chanel's spring 1927 collection also included a three-piece costume which consisted of a pleated skirt and jacket of navy-blue wool jersey and a blouse of rough, red silk and wool crepe striped with blue satin which was also used for the jacket lining. A suit from her 1929 collection was made of honeycomb-textured tweed in burnt orange with beaver collar and cuffs, and had a blouse of orange, beige and brown striped jersey. In 1929 Chanel produced a range of wool jersey caps and scarves, which were purchased by both men and women for winter sports.

During the late 1920s and early 1930s there was a great vogue for horizontally striped fabrics and these featured in many of Chanel's collections, woven at Tissus Chanel.

Poiret critically described Chanel's Garçonne Look as 'poverty de luxe' which has since been much quoted in reference to her fashions – some went as far as to describe it as a 'soup kitchen style'. Chanel however retorted that it was idiotic to confuse simplicity with poverty and had no doubts about the understated, luxurious elegance of her clothes.

In 1926 Chanel introduced her now legendary 'little black dresses'. The use of black for dress dates back some 500 years, but never before had it been used purely for its elegance and flattering qualities. Chanel's headline-making black dresses were made from wool or marocain for the day and dull silk crepe, satin, satin-backed crepe – utilising both the dull and shiny sides – and plain, printed and cut silk velvet for evening wear. Many of these evening garments were designed with luxurious jewelled and rhinestone-studded belts and eyelets. In American Vogue's issue of 1 October 1926, the editorial compared the design of Chanel's black dresses to the mass-produced Ford motor-car, emphasising how these designs would become standard wear for the masses.

For evening, Chanel designed a confection of lace dresses, using black lace combined with beige, metal embroidered lace, gold lace embroidered with turquoise beads, and laces in silver, pink or green. These were cut tight at the hips, sometimes with tiered skirts or with winged draperies on both bodice and skirt. She also created many dresses with partial or solid beading on silk and tulle grounds, which were often cut in one piece to avoid side seams.

During the 1920s Chanel was strongly influenced by Fair Isle knitwear and geometric designs and these motifs are evident in the decoration of many of her beaded evening dresses, as well as for her daywear. Chanel also designed

Chanel day ensemble, c1927

Checked silk dress and black crepe coat with matching lining – one of Chanel's signature combinations. The dress fastens at the front with three silk-covered buttons, has buttoned cuffs and three box pleats at the front. The coat has a matching scarf and all of the external coat seams are hand finished with two rows of decorative stitching.

some dramatic beaded dresses in combinations of black, gold and red which, with their straight shape and colouring, made them evocative of the lacquered screens she so loved.

In 1926 and 1927 some of Chanel's evening dresses were cut straight to a stiffened flounce at the hem. She made a feature of using triangular, square and rectangular scarves with her evening wear, as she had for daytime sports clothes. These could be worn draped around the neck and shoulders or left to hang freely and trail down the front of her clothes. In 1927 she created an interesting effect by crossing scarves or bands across the décolletage, both in front and at the back. Fashion in 1927 was characterised by the uneven hemline, as once again there was uncertainty about the length. This time Chanel was no exception and produced several evening dresses which were longer at the back than the front. She recognised that by raising the line of the waist at the front of a garment a woman appears taller and lowering it at the back is flattering.

White georgette evening dress with beading and and swags of fringing designed by Chanel in the early 1920s

Fringing was popular for evening wear as it created movement and emphasised the exuberance of the dance styles.

The Ranee of Pudakota wearing a Chanel suit, 1926

This three-piece cardigan suit consists of a checked jacket and skirt with a long sweater and scarf, both of which are finished with matching checked fabric. The Ranee of Pudakota is clearly comfortable in this stylish, understated suit which she wears with a cloche hat pulled deep down over the brow as was fashionable.

In 1929 Jean Patou was the first couturier to drop his hemline dramatically and return the waist to its natural position. The other houses followed suit and by September *Vogue* reported that:

'...when Chanel, the sponsor of the straight, chemise dress and the boyish silhouette, uses little, rippling capes on her fur coats and a high waist-line and numerous ruffles on an evening gown, then you may be sure that the feminine mode is a fact and not a fancy'.
(British *Vogue*, 4 September 1929, p.14)

They were absolutely correct.

CHANEL DESIGNS FOR THE STAGE

From the early 1920s Chanel became a great patron of the arts by providing financial assistance for her friends, many of whom were the leading musicians and artists of the day. In particular she supported the avant-garde writer and artist Jean Cocteau. In a bid to refurbish the classics during the summer of 1922, Jean Cocteau wrote an adaptation of Sophocles' *Antigone*, and Chanel agreed to design the costumes. She designed Grecian-style costumes in coarse undyed wool for the actors to wear. The Greek actress, Genica Althanasiou, played Antigone and had her hair cropped short, whitened her face and wore thick black kohl around her eyes. Chanel designed and had made for her a full-length coat hand-knitted in undyed wool with Greek vase motifs in maroon and black. However, in an angry moment during a rehearsal, when Chanel felt that her contribution was being overlooked, she grabbed a strand and started to unravel the coat, to the utter dismay of the onlooking knitter. There was not time to rectify the destruction and Antigone appeared wearing one of Chanel's own coats.

Chanel designed a gold headband encrusted with jewels for Charles Dullin, who was also director, to wear in his role as Creon. This may have been her first experience in the medium of jewellery which she was soon to develop so successfully. Picasso was also involved in the design of this production, being responsible for the sets and actors' masks and shields.

Antigone was premiered at the Théâtre de l'Atelier in Montmartre in December

Left: Chanel with Martha Davelli, 1929

Chanel was instrumental in gaining social acceptance for women to wear trousers, although it was still considered very daring, even for beach wear, during the 1920s. Here Chanel and her friend wear loose cut, sailor-style trousers with short-sleeved tops and flat sandals.

Lace evening dress by
Chanel, 1928 (left)

This magazine illustration
depicts a mauve lace dress
with a flaring skirt, stiffened
with bands of horsehair,
accessorised with a diamanté
belt clasp. This dropped-waist
Garçonne-style dress features
the trailing scarf which
completed many of Chanel's
ensembles during the 1920s.
It has an uneven hemline
which was particularly
fashionable in 1927 and 1928.

Illustration of Chanel's
Garçonne-style daywear, 1928

The two-piece outfit on the
left consists of a tucked
waistcoat and dress with
pleated collar in violet jersey.
The three-piece (central)
ensemble illustrates a beige
jersey skirt and cardigan style
jacket, lined with the same
geometric patterned jersey in
beige, rust, brown and black
as the sweater worn beneath.
The outfit on the right is of
beige-grey jersey banded with
black and beige and worn with
a scarf of black, yellow, beige
and white to match the
drop-waisted, striped belt.

EN VILLE

CHANEL OPENS THE WAY TO CHARM

Chanel has the rare gift of giving to the clothes she designs a pleasant feeling of
   friendliness. Take the sympathetic simplicity of this two-piece of violet jersey,
with its tucked sleeveless cardigan, and round pleated collar. There is the Chanel
colour appeal in this suit where a jumper of beige, rust, brown and black sparkles amidst
the beige of the coat and skirt. And what surer touch of genius than to put the band of
black and beige to hem the beige-grey walking suit, catching up the same colour not only
by the scarf of black, yellow, beige, and white, but in the striped belt of the same tones?

1922. Previews praised the protagonists' contemporary, if rather unconventional,
interpretation of antiquity. The fashion press paid particular attention to Chanel's
costumes and French *Vogue* featured them in its issue of 1 February 1923.

Chanel also became a sponsor of the Ballets Russes, which was directed by Serge
Diaghilev. Chanel first met Diaghilev when she accompanied the Serts on their
honeymoon trip to Venice and heard his concern about the Ballets' lack of funds
to re-stage *Le Sacré du Printemps*. She later arranged to meet him and offered
financial assistance.

Early in 1924 Chanel was invited to design the costumes for Diaghilev's Ballets
Russes performance of *Le Train Bleu*. This was première in June that year, at the
Théâtre des Champs-Elysées. The theme drew on the contemporary vogue for
sporting activities and imagery, featuring tennis, golf and swimming. The dance title
was taken from the name of the luxurious train, equipped with Lalique glass
accessories, which ran from Paris to Deauville and had made its maiden trip the
previous year.

Diaghilev hardly considered *Le Train Bleu* to be a ballet and instead described it as an *operetta dansée* which combined acrobatics, satire and pantomime. In this production he sought to inaugurate a new era of Modernist realism in dance. The musical score was composed by Darius Milhaud, the libretto by Jean Cocteau, and Bronislava Nijinska, sister of the famous dancer Nijinsky, directed the choreography. Picasso designed the programme and signed the stage curtain, which was an enlargement of one of his recent paintings showing two large-limbed women running across the beach, which had been copied on to the curtain by Prince Schervachidze. The Cubist sculptor Henri Laurens designed the sets in fashionable neutral colours which embraced angular, sloping beach cabins and parasols dotted along a beach.

Chanel dressed the dancers in jersey bathing costumes and sports clothes, similar to those seen in her fashion collections and to those she wore herself. The tennis player was performed by Nijinska and was based on the French tennis champion, Suzanne Lenglen. She wore a white tennis dress and eyeshade. Woizikovski sported a Fair Isle jumper and plus fours to resemble the Prince of Wales dressed in his sporting clothes.

The fittings for the dancers took place in Chanel's workrooms in the rue Cambon. Sokolova, who danced the role of Perlouse, wrote,

'When I tried on my pink bathing-dress, which we all thought very daring, the question of what I was to wear on my head arose. Three women stood around me, binding my hair with various pieces of materials, until at last they decided on a dark suede. The neat little skull-cap they made for me set a fashion.'
(Richard Buckle, p.222)

Sokolova was a young British woman whose real name was Hilda Munnings; she was one of many British dancers Diaghilev employed during the 1920s who had assumed Russian names. On the morning of the first performance, when the first dress rehearsal had just finished, Chanel told Sokolova she would provide her with some accessories to complement her costume. Sokolova described how she wore large pearl stud earrings, which were soon to become another classic House trademark.

The practical and stylish costumes which Chanel created for this production reinforced her own fashions. The dancers, with their lean and agile bodies, personified the ideal 1920s Garçonne woman and showed Chanel's clothes to great advantage.

In May and June 1924 Chanel also designed costumes for a series of unconventional dance spectacles called *Les Soirées de Paris* which incorporated the talents of Jean Hugo, Cocteau, Picasso, Marie Laurençin, Satie and Massine. Comte Etienne de Beaumont rented the Théâtre de la Cigale and sponsored the production – his first experience in this sphere. De Beaumont was already famous for the lavish masked costume balls he held for the social and artistic élite of Paris, in his 18th-century mansion on the Boulevard des Invalides. In 1926 Cocteau again revived his interest in Greek tragedy by producing his version of *Orphée*, the romantic legend of Orpheus and Eurydice. This starred Ludmilla and Georges Pitoeff, who was also the show's director. Cocteau decreed that this was to be a contemporary performance and commissioned Jean Hugo to design the sets and Chanel the costumes. She dressed the actresses in her latest fashions.

Chanel's next work for the ballet came three years later, when she stepped in at the last minute to design some of the costumes for the Ballets Russes' *Apollon Musagètes*, for which Stravinsky composed the music. Initially the sets and costumes had been under the direction of Bauchant, but his difficult temperament lost him the job. While Diaghilev managed to improvise most of the costumes himself, he was unable to find suitable dress for the Muses. Chanel came quickly to the aid of her friend by again designing adaptations of the Greek tunic for these dancers to wear.

Scene from *Antigone*, 1922

Antigone was adapted by Jean Cocteau, the sets were by Picasso and Chanel designed the costumes which were inspired by classical Greek dress. Here Genica Althanasiou (right) plays Antigone wearing a heavy cape of brown wool. Photograph by Wladimir Rehbinder for *Vogue. Vogue* wrote, 'These woollen clothes in neutral tones look like antique garments rediscovered after centuries.'

Chanel necklace, 1925-1935

Clusters of pearls form this star necklace which has an individual pearl pendant at the tip of each of the five points and at the end of the pendant clasp.

Chanel's bird brooches, 1925-1935

Stylised brooches of birds whose plumage, eyes and feet are highlighted with red glass stones and diamanté.

Scene from *Le Train Bleu*, 1924

Diaghilev's Ballets Russes performed this *operetta dansée* which was inspired by the vogue for sporting activities. Lydia Sokolova in the role of Perlouse wears Chanel's woollen bathing costume and Léon Woizikovski's sporting dress is based on that worn by the Prince of Wales.

JEWELLERY

During the early 1920s Chanel introduced luxurious costume jewellery which she herself wore in abundance. The simple shapes and predominantly plain fabrics of her garments formed an ideal ground to offset her costume jewellery. Chanel was not the first to make artificial gemstones: imitative jewellery dates back to ancient Egyptian times when coated glass beads were used to resemble precious stones. Nor was she the first couturière to diversify, although traditionally the design of costume jewellery had followed that of precious jewels. In contrast, Chanel's *faux* gems were proudly and defiantly fake and she was the first to gain them social acceptability among a clientèle who could afford and already owned priceless jewels. Equally, the fame and respect attached to the House of Chanel ensured that her designs acquired prestige and desirability and their high price ensured exclusivity.

Chanel adored jewellery, but always advocated that it should be worn to decorate rather than to flaunt wealth. She believed that if a woman wore a lot of jewellery, it was important that it be fake, that there was nothing more foolish than women dripping with real jewels. She said that too much money killed luxury.

In spite of the fact that Chanel owned a magnificent collection of valuable jewels, much of which she had received as gifts from her wealthy lovers, she rarely wore them. Instead, she broke all established conventions about how and when jewellery should be worn. She wore heaps of jewellery during the daytime, even for such informal occasions as sailing and spending time on the beach. Traditionally, women would have worn a minimal amount of discreet jewellery in daylight. Conversely, in the evening Chanel often wore no jewellery at all. Although she did not generally use

Chanel was the first designer
to gain social acceptance for
costume jewellery, which she
wore in abundance with her
understated daywear. Her
jewellery workshops produced
masses of fake pearls which
defied nature in size and
colour and have remained
popular to the present day.

precious materials – Chanel was known occasionally to mix real and imitation stones – her jewellery was still extremely expensive. As with her clothes, however, the designs were widely copied in cheaper forms.

Chanel designed much of the jewellery herself, creating larger-than-life versions of her own precious jewellery collection. The Romanov jewels given to her by Dmitri inspired her to create long ropes of gilt chains hung with Baroque pearls and *pâte de verre* crosses. Her magnificent jewels given by the Duke of Westminster also provided her with endless ideas. On one occasion the duke had presented her with superb bracelets of rare Indian emeralds, rubies and sapphires, which she felt were too ostentatious. She told him, with characteristic frankness, that she would prefer them if they were taken out of their settings. Chanel subsequently designed much of her costume jewellery by arranging and rearranging these stones on a flexible base.

Chanel opened her own jewellery workshops in 1924 and appointed Comte Etienne de Beaumont as manager. Chanel was proud that she was independent and earned her own living and never hesitated to ask the aristocracy to work for her. Although he had not worked professionally in this line, the Comte had had his own designs made up at Maison Gripoix to give as personal presents and subsequently much of Chanel's jewellery was manufactured there. It was de Beaumont who designed the long chains with coloured stones, sometimes with a cross pendant, which have remained a House classic. Instead of securing the stone into a base, a band of metal was formed around the edge of each to allow greater translucency. This method has been used by the House of Chanel ever since and has become a trade standard. Chanel also occasionally asked François Hugo, who was then director of her jersey factory in Asnières, to design jewellery for her during the 1920s.

Mme Gripoix and her husband were famous costume jewellers, renowned for their work in *pâte de verre* and enamels and for their fine execution of naturalistic forms. Gripoix and other costume jewellers had become established in Paris during the early 1900s when there existed a huge demand for convincing replica jewellery, both for the stage and among a private clientèle. Gripoix had also made costume jewellery for Poiret, who was the first couturier to design costume jewellery to complement his fashion collections. Thus, when Chanel decided to diversify into this area, there already existed a network of manufacturers and suppliers to whom she could turn for support. Gripoix had a very high reputation and continually mastered new techniques of making and setting jewellery. Throughout the 1920s and 1930s Chanel regularly used Venetian patterned glass beads, which Gripoix incorporated into her jewellery. Gripoix remains a family-run business and continues to work for the House of Chanel.

Chanel's inspiration for her jewellery was eclectic, although a great many pieces were inspired by the exotic and oriental. In common with many designers, Chanel was inspired by Egyptian design which was brought to public attention following the opening of Tutankhamen's tomb late in 1922. She was also fascinated by the rich jewels produced during the Renaissance and Byzantine periods and visited the Schatzkammer collection in Munich which held fine original examples. The Byzantine crosses encrusted with heavy stones were among her favourite items and she regularly produced costume versions of these. Chanel's jewellery was also inspired by the buttons, chains and tassels which adorned military uniforms. From the mid 1920s Chanel became renowned for adding masses of rows of fake pearls – sometimes fastened by huge coloured Maharajah-style coloured stones – chokers, brooches and pendants to her understated fashions. In 1926 she created a vogue for mismatched earrings by herself wearing a black pearl in one ear and a white in the other. During Chanel's youth pearls had been one of the most costly and precious stones, which were conspicuously worn by wealthy socialites and aristocrats. There consequently existed a large trade for fake pearls for those unable to afford the real thing. The best imitation pearls were made in France and were often called Paris pearls. During the inter-war years fake pearls were often made from glass or plastic which was covered with *essence d'Orient*, an iridescent material extracted from fish scales. Chanel emphasised the artificiality of her pearls by producing them in sizes and colours which defied nature.

During the late 1920s much of her jewellery was made using multi-coloured semi-precious stones, such as amethyst, topaz and aquamarine, which were cut flat and set in silver or gold metal, with bracelets and rings to match. She also introduced a distinctive crystal pin to be worn with her evening dresses. This consisted of several long drops of crystal with star-shaped motifs at the end. In 1928 the House launched a range of diamond paste jewellery created by Comte Etienne de Beaumont. In 1929 Chanel produced a series of gypsy necklaces – triple strands of red, green and yellow beads and also red stones and turquoise beads with chunky wooden chains.

Many of the jewellery designs which Chanel produced during the 1920s have since become classics. Similar pieces regularly reappear in Chanel collections to the present day and continue to influence the jewellery trade.

DISSEMINATION OF THE CHANEL STYLE

'Fashion does not exist unless it goes down into the streets. The fashion that remains in the salons has no more significance than a costume ball.' Chanel (Edmonde Charles Roux, 1981, p.237)

During the 1920s, as never before, the essence of haute couture could be translated for the fashion-hungry mass market. There were several reasons for this. The simple, loose shapes of Chanel's suits and dresses overcame sizing problems in manufacture. Most of her garments required a minimal amount of fabric, just two to three metres, and were virtually straight in cut and thus easy to copy in cheap fabrics.

Furthermore, Chanel's use of lower-priced textiles, such as jersey, made versions of her fashions more accessible. The improved quality of synthetic fibres in the 1920s, such as rayon, which superficially resembled the appearance and feel of natural silk, also enabled manufacturers to copy luxurious silk couture garments at a fraction of the price.

At last, high fashion had become functional and was as well suited to the mass of working women and housewives as to the privileged patrons of haute couture. Chanel had clear views about her role as a designer and felt that the dissemination of her designs was vital to her success. She was also well aware that the cut and quality of her own clothes could never be mistaken for cheaper ready-to-wear copies.

The direct copying of couture models was undertaken at the top end of the clothing trade, that is by department stores and exclusive dress shops. A small group or an individual representative would attend the Paris shows to keep up-to-date with the latest seasonal trends. Some would purchase toiles with the express intention of emulating their design. Others, indeed the vast majority, would unofficially copy the collections by surreptitiously drawing what they saw on the catwalks and inspected at close quarters backstage when they posed as buyers. Back at their hotel they could make accurate sketches of the models seen and speedily ship them to be copied at home.

Specialist copy houses also existed. In the mid 1920s Elizabeth Hawes worked for a high-class copy house owned by Mme Doret, who had premises in Faubourg St Honoré in the centre of the Parisian couture district. In her memoirs, *Fashion is Spinach*, Hawes recalls that many people wanted Chanel clothes but could not afford them and the company she worked for helped to fill this gap (Elizabeth Hawes, p.41). Mme Doret obtained her designs by sending Hawes, who was American, to the couture houses to pose as a customer and purchase models which were then copied. She also obtained them from customers, who would lend their original garments in return for copies of other items, and from resident American buyers, such as Mme Ellis, before they were despatched abroad. Hawes describes how one

Chanel photographed in 1929. Her straw cloche hat is accessorised with a satin band and large pearl-ended hatpins.

Chanel wearing one of her classic three-piece jersey costumes, 1929 (left) and Chanel with Vera Bate (right)

This was the look that Poiret dubbed '*Poverty de luxe*'. Because of the simplicity of style and use of more durable fabrics, Chanel's designs could be successfully translated for the fashion-hungry mass market during the 1920s.

day she was sent to Ellis's office, where she was given some Chanel models which she was told to hide under her coat and return with them as speedily as possible. Hawes fled back to the workrooms where patterns were made and sample fabrics snipped from the seams so that an accurate match could be achieved. As a result of this illicit deal, Mme Doret had eight new 'Chanel' models to sell.

Retail outlets also proudly promoted the fact that they would copy Paris models for a fraction of the original cost. In British *Vogue*, May 1926, an advertisement was placed by the exclusive dressmaker Cecile, whose premises were at 63 South Molton Street, London W1. She announced that she was showing many models, including Chanel's, which she would copy from just 11 guineas (£11.55). French and American *Vogue* also carried similar advertisements.

The cheaper end of the trade would in turn copy the version marketed by the more exclusive companies. Many copies of Chanel's clothes were also made from illustrations and photographs in fashion magazines. By these means the major elements of the most exclusive couture garments filtered through to the cheapest

mass-produced clothes. Chanel represented an exception among couturiers because she was flattered that her styles were so popular and widely copied. She would not, however, endorse copyists illegally sketching her designs and was renowned for having her guests watched like hawks during her shows.

On one occasion Chanel did invite dressmakers and manufacturers to directly copy her models in order to raise funds for the War Service Legion, which had been founded in 1918 by Lady Londonderry and Lady Titchfield. Chanel decided to show her fashions in the form of an exhibition in a house provided for her use by the Duke of Westminster at 39 Grosvenor Square, London. She presented 130 designs, all made from British fabrics. The exhibition opened on 6 May 1932 and was immensely popular. The daily newspapers described how women attended in their hordes accompanied by their dressmakers, ready to copy these items with Chanel's official sanction. Needless to say, manufacturers from all over England also attended.

Designers, manufacturers and stylists continue to exploit the Chanel look to the present day.

Three THE 1930s

Following the collapse of the Wall Street stock market in 1929, the United States and Europe suffered a depression which dramatically hit the luxury trades, including fashion. The American buyers, who had formed such a large part of the couture houses' clientèle during the 1920s, cancelled orders which had already been executed and few came to the mid-December Paris shows. In 1925 unemployment in the French fashion industry had been rare but in 1929, as a direct result of the Depression, some 10,000 workers were laid off as international demand for haute couture clothing decreased.

Although Chanel lost some business she retained her lucrative Indian and South American markets and continued to dress an international wealthy and fashionable élite. Daisy Fellowes remained a customer and Lady Pamela Smith, Laura Corrigan, Barbara Hutton and Diana Vreeland as well as the South American beauty Martinez de Hoz were among her many clients during the 1930s.

In 1930 Chanel had a turnover of around 120 million francs and employed some 2,400 staff in her 26 workrooms. Chanel's income was further boosted by her work in Hollywood during 1931 and 1932, for which she earned two million dollars. It has been stated that she was compelled to cut her prices in half in 1932 (Georgina Howell, p.104) but whatever the case her business continued to expand. By 1935 she employed some 4,000 workers. From 1935 to 1939 a number of famous costume balls were held in Paris which necessitated lavish couture clothing and which boosted business considerably. Worldwide demand for her perfumes led to the expansion of the range to include No. 22, Glamour and Gardenia – although it was No. 5 which remained the top seller. She also branched into the production of cosmetics. The Duke of Westminster, who remained a close friend after his marriage to Loelia Ponsonby in 1930, let Chanel use, and adapted to her requirements, his nine-bedroom London house at 9 South Audley Street, rent-free. It became the headquarters of the Chanel cosmetics venture from 1930 to 1934.

Although she was highly successful Chanel, in common with many couturiers of this period, endorsed products and designed clothing and textiles for manufacturers as a means of gaining extra publicity and raising revenue. In 1931 she was invited to London to promote cotton dress fabrics by Ferguson Brothers Ltd of Carlisle. As a result, her 1931 spring collection included 35 evening dresses made from cotton piqué, lawn, muslin and organdie, which had been traditionally considered too informal for evening wear. In 1933 Chanel produced designs for several British manufacturers including jumpers for Ellaness, a Scottish knitwear

CHANEL: THE COUTURIERE AT WORK

Chanel's apartment at the Paris Ritz, 1937

Chanel did not sketch her designs, preferring instead to work with fabric directly on the body. These working drawings would have been executed by her employees as references for making up her clothes and for publicity purposes.

For the first time you can buy Chanel's model silks in a shop in London in the same season in which she shows them in Paris. Here are six from a collection, which Chanel, who doesn't need to boast, told us is one of her very best. We invite you to see Chanel's collection shown for the first time in London. And happily you will find her silks priced from 6/11 per yard.

Harvey Nichols of Knightsbridge

.... the incomparable Chanel says "Harvey Nichols are the people in London who are to sell my Model Silks".......

CHANEL
31, RUE CAMBON · PARIS

I am sure that English women will be enthusiastic about the new prints which I have created for this season. I have selected very carefully for Harvey Nichols, some of the designs which I, myself, like best, and which I think will meet the tastes of the English woman. There is one trend which I should like to mention --- according to my idea, it is the material that makes the dress and not the ornaments that one can add.

Harvey Nichols are to have in their Silk Department three or four of my original models carried out in the new Prints for Spring. I am sure that when women see these, they will find it both easy and fascinating to decide upon the materials and the model which they will want for themselves.

Gabrielle Chanel

Textile designs by Chanel for Harvey Nichols, 1939

It was during the 1930s that fashion designers started to design and license their names to shops and manufacturers to raise additional revenue and publicity. Here Harvey Nichols proudly advertise in *Vogue* their range of printed silks, in small rather naive designs, by the famous Parisian couturière Gabrielle Chanel.

company who boasted of their alliance with the world famous couturière in their advertising. The jumpers were made from textured tweed yarns in striped and spotted patterns. They ended at the waist and had lean fitted sleeves, although one design was puffed just above the elbow. In the same year David Moseley & Sons Ltd of Margaret Street, London, advertised their range of sportscoats and rainwear designed by Chanel.

FASHION 1930 TO 1935

Women's clothing in the 1930s rejected the angular severity of the previous decade. Although fashion remained slender in form, garments were designed to follow and accentuate, rather than deny the bust, waist and hips. This was achieved with smooth textiles, such as satin weaves which were cut on the bias to enable the fabric to follow the lines of the body without wrinkles or creases. The bodices of many dresses became slightly bloused, tight belts emphasised the waist and, below the hips, garments gradually widened. An inset godet added fullness at the hem. Similarly, Chanel's suit jackets had soft, bloused bodices which created an effect of fullness which was accentuated by her use of cravat bows, making the waistline look even smaller. By the mid 1930s this look was exaggerated by the use of shoulder pads. Hemlines for day wear reached six inches from the ground and were returned to full-length for evening.

For day and evening wear Chanel started to use crisp frills around collars and cuffs in a strongly contrasting colour, often white on a black suit or dress. This look was to become one of her many signatures. Black and white formed the mainstay of her day wear collections with hints of red, green, brown and amethyst, with mustard-brown being much used for sportswear and coats. From 1934 Chanel used the new American Lastex (later called Latex) elasticated fabrics in her collections. These ranged from fabrics which resembled the appearance of crepe to

Chanel with group of mannequins, 1930s. Photograph by Roger Schall

Chanel personified her House style. Here she is photographed with a group of house mannequins whose dark looks reinforced her own. Several of the models wear Chanel's signature bow in their hair.

those that were combined with her favourite jersey fabrics. Prices for Chanel day wear were in the range of 1,600 to 1,900 francs. (Journal, 1.4.35 p.2)

Far from reflecting the financial depression of the 1930s, fashions in evening wear revelled in femininity, luxury and extravagance. Black velvet berets and short top hats were designed to be worn with her luxurious black velvet capes, many of which were dramatically lined with red or white fabric. She also used gold satin lamé as a glamorous evening dress fabric and trim. Evening wear throughout the 1930s was dominated by the use of white, cream and peach coloured satins and Chanel's collections were no exception. In 1931 she designed a full-length evening dress in white satin and rose chiffon with poufes at the back, possibly anticipating the revival of Victorian bustle styles later in the decade. By 1934 Chanel had largely abandoned trains on her evening gowns in favour of a shorter or more body-moulding line, which often flared from the hip or from the knee. It was during the 1930s that she started regularly to incorporate bows, both as decorative motifs and as applied decoration on shoulders and down the fronts and backs of her skirts.

Multi-coloured wool jersey suit by Chanel, 1930 - 1935

The long woven jersey jacket with scarf collar has no buttons or fastenings. The cuffs and two large patch pockets are lined with yellow jersey. The yoked skirt is pleated from the hips. Beneath the jacket the bodice of yellow jersey is made like a man's waistcoat with four pockets and button fastenings.

THE STRIKE AT THE HOUSE OF CHANEL

On 26 April 1936, the Popular Front gained a majority in the French Parliament and Léon Blum succeeded Albert Sarraut as Prime Minister. As the defeated National Assembly did not officially leave office until the end of May, Blum did not take over

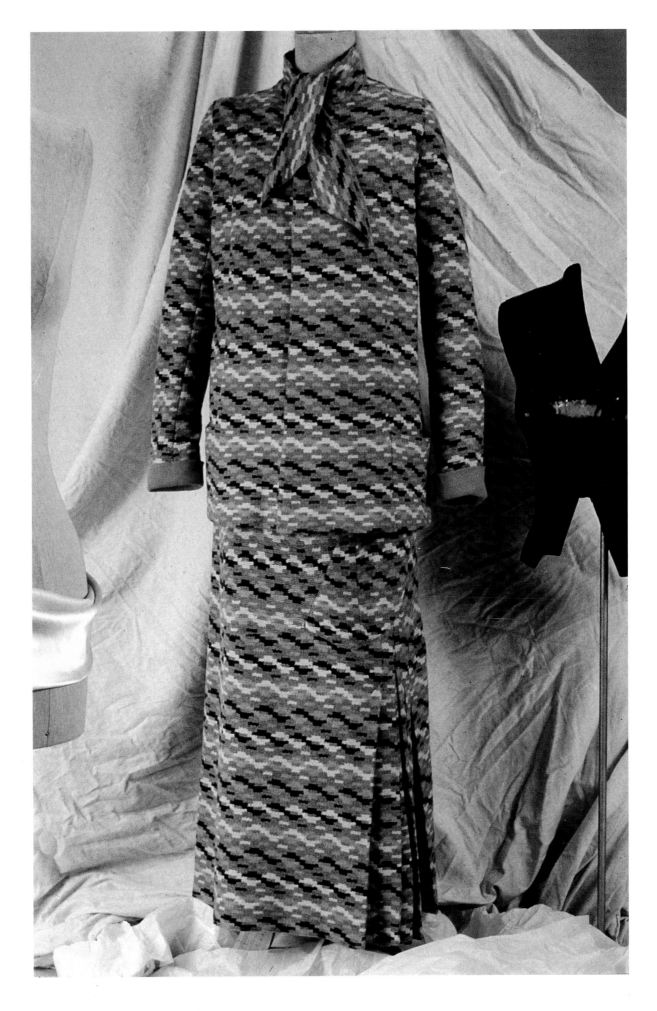

Detail of Chanel's evening dress worn by the Duchess of Westminster, 1932

This full-length, body-moulding blue sequinned evening dress flares from below the hips. It has Chanel's signature bow appliquéd at the front, while the ties hang freely.

Victoria & Albert Museum, London (T.339-1960)

Chanel beach outfit, 1930s

These beach trousers with shoulder straps worn over a matching bra top look remarkably contemporary.

until June. During this interim period, France was devastated by a wave of unofficial strikes and industry was brought to a standstill as workers fought for better working conditions.

On 8 June the Matignon Agreement was signed by many employers agreeing to reduce the working week to 40 hours and introduce paid holidays. At first Chanel refused to implement this for the benefit of her own workers, who were also demanding proper contracts and weekly salaries. This was important as contracts were often seasonal in the fashion trades and job insecurity was very high during the 1930s. Tension grew when she sacked 300 of her workers, but she finally relented, following the advice of her lawyer, René de Chambrun, and her financial directors who informed her that, unless a solution was quickly reached, she would be unable to present her autumn collection.

CHANEL DESIGNS FOR THE SCREEN AND STAGE

In 1929 Dmitri introduced Chanel to Samuel Goldwyn, the Hollywood magnate, in Monaco. The Depression had led to a drop in cinema box office figures and Goldwyn was looking for a way to revive attendances. He saw in Chanel the opportunity to entice his female audience with the allure of Paris fashions, acknowledging that women went to the cinema for the stars and the story, but also to see the clothes. From the outset of her career Chanel's millinery and clothing designs had been promoted on stage and off by the leading actresses of the day.

Goldwyn hoped not only to keep abreast of Paris fashions but actually to be at the forefront of the latest trends. The need to keep up with Paris fashion had recently been brought to a head when thousands of reels of film had had to be discarded because Patou unexpectedly lengthened his hemlines in 1929 and was promptly followed by his colleagues. This rendered film already shot instantly old-fashioned. In an attempt to overcome such problems the studios sent scores of stylists to Paris to inform them of the latest fashion trends. Goldwyn's solution was even better – to bring a world-acclaimed Parisian couturière to Hollywood. Chanel was famous for

Portrait of Chanel by Lipnitzki, 1935

Chanel wears an 1870s-style dress at one of Comte Etienne de Beaumont's famous costume balls. The graduated layers of tulle on her dress create an impression of a bustle and the black plumed hat, lace gloves and fan reinforce this vogue for late 19th-century revival styles. As a young woman Chanel had rebelled against the frou frou of the early 20th century, but by the late 1930s enjoyed her own forays into extravagant dress.

Gloria Swanson in *Tonight or Never*, 1931

Samuel Goldwyn invited Chanel to Hollywood to design the on- and off-screen wardrobes for his stars. However, while her under-stated, stylish clothes were a huge hit in Europe and America, they were widely considered not to be sensational enough for Hollywood.

bring a world-acclaimed Parisian couturière to Hollywood. Chanel was famous for the simplicity of her designs which would not date as quickly as the clothes of many other couture houses. A film often took a year or more to make and the costumes could not look dated when it was released.

Goldwyn also wanted to reform the notoriously extravagant tastes in dress enjoyed by many actresses. As a result of the Depression, companies had to deal with tighter budgets. In addition, sound, which had been introduced in 1929, removed the handicap of striving for theatrical effects alone. As a result of the constraints on the one hand and the new freedom on the other, Hollywood's film costumes gradually moved away from theatricality towards high fashion. The employment of a couturière, accustomed to providing more discreet dress than was usually seen on the screens, seemed ideal. The plan was that Chanel would have a team of 50 staff permanently based in Hollywood to whom she would send new designs all year round, in addition to travelling to the film capital each spring and autumn herself.

Goldwyn offered Chanel $1 million a year to design two collections a year for the on- and off-screen wardrobes for MGM's stars, including Greta Garbo, Gloria Swanson, Marlene Dietrich and Claudette Colbert. After an initial hesitation Chanel finally agreed to Goldwyn's proposal, clearly recognising that this venture would increase her world fame and undoubtedly open her perfume sales to a new cinema-going market which could not afford her clothes.

This was not, however, a straightforward contract. In an article in the American magazine *Colliers*, Laura Mount anticipated the problems that Chanel would face:

'Chanel has picked herself the hardest job she has ever tackled. The world-famous fashion dictator who tells the duchesses and countesses and queens of Europe what to wear is now going to try and tell the duchesses and queens of the talkies. And it is just possible that in the talkies they may talk back.'

(Laura Mount, p.21)

Chanel as usual was confident of her own ability to succeed: she had already designed for the stage and was now keen to stretch her talents to create for the screen.

Chanel's much-publicised stay was, however, briefer than either she or Goldwyn had anticipated. She designed the costumes for just three Hollywood films: *Palmy Days* (1931) which was a musical comedy starring Charlotte Greenwood and Eddie Cantor, *Tonight or Never* (1931) which starred Gloria Swanson and *The Greeks Had a Word For It* (1932) starring Ina Claire.

For *Palmy Days* Chanel was given little scope and only designed a few dresses for Greenwood who played the role of a hyperactive gym instructor. In *Tonight or Never* Swanson played the role of a young concert singer who was engaged to an ageing nobleman, played by Ferdinand Gottschalk, but was infatuated with a young stranger, Melvyn Douglas, who it emerged was an impresario set on offering her an opera contract. Chanel was keen to return to her rue Cambon business and Goldwyn agreed that Swanson, who was in London for the première of her latest film *Indiscreet*, would travel back to America via Paris. In her autobiography, Swanson vividly recalls her experience with Mademoiselle:

'Coco Chanel, tiny and fierce, approaching fifty, wearing a hat, as she always did at work, glared furiously at me when I had trouble squeezing into one of the gowns she had measured me for six weeks earlier. It was black satin, cut on the bias, a great work in the eyes of both of us.'
(Gloria Swanson, p.414)

Swanson was actually pregnant, a fact she wished to remain a secret for as long as possible.

While *Tonight or Never* was being filmed, Chanel designed the costumes for a screen adaptation of Zoe Atkin's Broadway comedy *The Greeks Had a Word for It*, which was directed by Lowell Sherman. The film told the story of three rival gold-diggers, one of whom was Ina Claire who was famous for her elegant style of dress.

In spite of her initial determination to make a success of this project and Goldwyn's faith in her ability to do so, Chanel's costumes were overlooked or criticised for not being sensational enough. *Tonight or Never* was a box office failure and Chanel's clothes were given little press coverage. Although *The Greeks Had A Word for It* was a huge commercial hit, again Chanel's clothes were not reviewed. Furthermore, as Mount had predicted, many actresses refused to have the Chanel style imposed on them. She could not tolerate being subordinate to actresses and left Hollywood exasperated.

To supply the clothes for MGM's leading stars was clearly too great a task for any one designer, and the cinema and its stars demanded more obviously spectacular creations than Chanel could ever provide. From the early 1930s the studios lessened their direct dependence upon Paris by promoting the talents of the studio designers, who created their own versions of French fashions, as well as creating some independent styles of their own.

Although Chanel had been disillusioned by her experience in Hollywood she continued to enjoy designing for avant-garde French films directed by her friends Jean Renoir and Jean Cocteau.

In 1934 Chanel designed the costumes for Cocteau's *La Machine Infernale* which had sets designed by leading fashion illustrator, Christian Bérard, his first work in this area, and which was produced by Louis Jouvet. That year, Cocteau rediscovered the Arthurian legend of the Holy Grail and developed it into a new play called *Les Chevaliers de la Table Ronde* for which Chanel was again invited to create the costumes. This was first shown in 1937. In the same year Cocteau also revived *Oedipe-Roi* and for this production Chanel dressed the male dancers in Egyptian, mummy-

Chanel jewellery, 1930

Necklace of pearls and gold metal chain with chain and pearl droplet pendant. The brooch of gold metal makes a decorative feature of three of Chanel's interlinked double C insignia's, with a central pearl and a pearl on each of the three points. The earrings resemble a Paisley motif and are made of gold metal with pearls and dark coloured stones.

like wrappings, which revealed glimpses of the body. These were criticised by the press, which considered them to be indecent.

In 1938 Jean Renoir asked Chanel to design the wardrobes for his film *La Marseillaise*. The film was set during the French Revolution and was a comment upon the rights of the French people united against exploitation. It was supported by the recently revived leftist labour federation, the *Confédération Générale du Travail*. In spite of her dislike of left-wing politics, Chanel agreed.

She also designed the clothes for *La Règle du Jeu*, which also had sets by Christian Bérard, in 1939. This film, a satire about contemporary bourgeois society, was produced in five acts and had its roots in classical comedy. The storyline was about a large house-party gathering for a hunt where the masters and servants turn upon and shoot each other. The film was first seen by French audiences in July, when Hitler was threatening Poland. It was preceded by a documentary celebrating the glories of the French Empire, which was greeted by cheers from the audience. Renoir's film did not meet with the same approval. The audience was furious: they considered it to be unpatriotic and in poor taste and even tried to set fire to the chair in which Renoir was seated at the première. The film was subsequently banned by the censors for being demoralising.

JEWELLERY

In 1932 Chanel was invited to create a range of real diamond jewellery. In an attempt to boost their sales, the International Diamond Guild commissioned her to

Diamond and platinum open necklace, 1993

This comet necklace, based on the designs from the 1932 exhibition, has recently been re-launched by the House of Chanel.

design a range of jewellery to be shown in her own home in the rue du Faubourg Saint-Honoré. The exhibition was called Bijoux de Diamants. Chanel emphasised that she had created fake jewels in the first place because they were free of arrogance at a time when luxury was easy. Her theory now was that diamonds were an investment in times of Depression, not an extravagance.

Chanel worked on this project with illustrator and designer Paul Iribe with whom she had a romantic relationship from 1931 until his premature death in 1935. Iribe had designed jewellery for Cartier and was at the time working at the Tissus Chanel factory. Together, they presented a selection of diamonds which was based on three main design themes: knots, stars and feathers, motifs which had also been fashionable in the 18th century and were later revived from the 1860s to 1890s. Chanel and Iribe's jewellery was particularly noted for its extravagant use of diamonds with discreet mounts and lack of clasps and for the interchangeable pieces. Diamonds set in a curly feather shape with a long quill stem could be used either as a brooch or as a hair ornament while crescent-shaped necklaces with sunbursts and comets of

Portrait of Chanel by
Lipnitzki, 1936

Here Chanel wears, in
characteristic style, a plain dark
sweater adorned with masses
of pearl necklaces and also
wears bracelets and earrings.

diamonds could also be worn as tiaras. The necklaces were shaped to curve around the neck and did not close with a fastening. Diamond-studded bow-knots decorated many of the pieces and reinforced their use in Chanel's clothing.

The jewellery was exhibited on lifelike wax busts, each of which had a different facial expression, and stood on a black marble stand. Some of the models were draped with luxurious fur wraps fastened with diamond clips, which instantly created a fashion for wearing jewellery with heavy fur coats. A lavish catalogue was produced to promote the event with a text by Chanel and photographs by film-maker Robert Bresson. An entrance fee was charged to raise money for the Charité Maternelle, founded in 1784, which had enjoyed the support of Marie Antoinette. It had been hoped that the exhibition would travel to London and to Ireland to raise money for the Personal Service League for Distressed Areas, of which the Queen was a patron. However, this was not possible as customs officials demanded that a prohibitive 30 per cent duty be charged on the value of the jewellery.

During the 1930s Chanel added another aristocratic figure to her staff of

Chanel with Fulco Santo Stefano della Cerda, Duke of Verdura, photographed by Lipnitzki

During the 1930s the Duke designed some of Chanel's most exciting jewellery and pioneered the revival of baked enamel. Here he is pictured showing Chanel one of his baked enamel bracelets decorated with multi-coloured stones in the form of an eight pointed Maltese cross. Chanel regularly wore one of these on each wrist.

Chanel jewellery, late 1930s

From the late 1930s some of
Chanel's designs were inspired
by Indian jewellery, of which
she had a fine collection

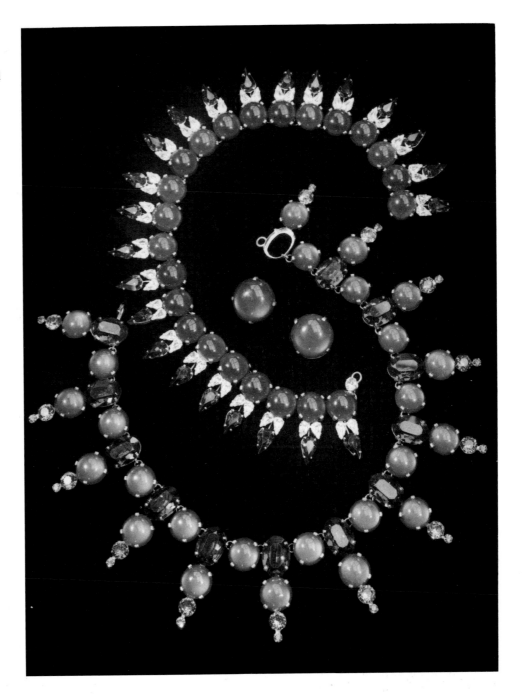

jewellery designers. Fulco Santo Stefano della Cerda, Duke of Verdura, designed
some of Chanel's most innovative and stylish jewellery. Indeed, many of his designs
were put back into production when Chanel reopened her House in 1954. The duke
left Sicily in 1927, the year after the death of his father. Planning to become a painter
he travelled to Paris, the metropolis of the arts. Soon after arriving he was employed
by Chanel as a textile designer and was soon promoted to head her jewellery
workshop. Verdura had a great historical knowledge which he drew upon to create an
eclectic range of jewellery which featured motifs based upon Classical, Medieval and
Baroque forms.

While he worked for Chanel, Verdura became famous for his fine designs and in
particular for pioneering the revival of baked enamel in rich colours. One of his first
projects was the design of black and white enamel bracelets, which were decorated
with multicoloured stones in the form of the eight-pointed Maltese cross. These
bracelets were clearly inspired by the ivory bracelets in the Bavarian Royal Collection
in Munich. Verdura produced many variations of this popular design for Chanel. In
the mid 1930s Verdura moved to New York, where he briefly designed for the

jeweller Paul Flato and in 1937 he set up on his own.

Christian Bérard also designed occasional pieces of jewellery for Chanel but worked more frequently for Schiaparelli. Throughout the 1930s much of Chanel's jewellery continued to be made at Maison Gripoix and to exploit popular Rococo motifs and naturalistic imagery. From 1937 there was a revival of late 19th-century styles, which was particularly evident in furnishing and fashion design. To complement these fashions there emerged a profusion of jewellery in floral and foliate forms and Chanel designed many simple flower spray brooches in coloured stones and enamels during these years. Brooches in the form of bouquets of anemones in red and blue stones with gilt stems and garland brooches of anemones in pink crystal and red cabochon appeared in her 1938 range. She also created floral earrings made from clusters of multicoloured stones and designed a dryad necklace of green oak leaves and yellow acorns decorated with coloured enamels in 1938.

From the mid to late 1930s Chanel's jewellery designs were inspired by Indian and South East Asian sources. Particularly popular were her heavy triangular bibs of coloured stones and coins which cascaded down the neck, supported by metal chains. In 1939 these bib necklaces were sometimes sewn directly on to dresses. Silk cord necklaces which were tied, Hindu style, with dangling tassels of brilliant coloured stones falling down the back were also a House favourite.

FASHION 1936 TO 1939

During the 1930s Chanel's most notable Parisian competitors included Elsa Schiaparelli and Madeleine Vionnet. Although Schiaparelli was admired for her understated and elegant garments, she was best known for the challenging and witty surreal designs she created in conjunction with Salvador Dali and other Surrealists from the mid to late 1930s. Aquatic imagery was much loved by the Surrealists and Chanel's white grosgrain shell hat of 1938 and colourful enamelled seahorse brooches of around this date subtly reinforced the more decorative elements of this movement. In stark contrast to the work of Schiaparelli, Vionnet was renowned for the visual simplicity of her bias-cut day and evening wear and her fluid garments inspired by classical sources.

(Above, left) Chanel by François Kollar, 1937

Here Chanel wears a belted tailored jacket with a gold wire belt, one of Verdura's enamel bracelets embellished with a Maltese cross and a gold and topaz ring.

(Above, right) Chanel by François Kollar, 1937

This portrait of Chanel on the telephone and with an accordion shows off her jewellery to great advantage. She wears baked enamel bracelets by Verdura and an emerald and diamond necklace.

Portrait of Chanel by Roger Schall, 1938

Chanel wears a sailor hat with a large jewelled brooch and masses of pearls with her striped jersey.

Detail of Chanel's trouser suit
worn by Diana Vreeland,
1937-8

This evening ensemble
consists of a sequinned trouser
suit and short sleeved blouse
of cream silk chiffon and lace,
fastened with pearl buttons.
The tailored bolero jacket and
straight-cut, high-waisted
trousers are entirely covered
with overlapping sequins
sewn in vertical rows. The
glimmering black of the
trouser suit, which resembles
gleaming metal, contrasts
dramatically with the soft
ruffles of the (entirely hand-
made) blouse. The outfit was
originally accessorised with a
black ribbon tied around the
neck, into which a red rose
was placed.

Victoria & Albert Museum,
London (T.87 & A-1974)

Evening dress and cape
worn by Mrs Leo D'Arlanger,
1937-8

Much of Chanel's evening
wear in the 1930s was in this
dramatic colour combination.
This ensemble consists of a
full-length dress covered with
black sequins, applied in the
fish-scale manner, with scarlet
silk satin panels and sashes.
The bodice is sleeveless with
narrow shoulder straps. The
matching semi circular cape
can be caught at the neck with
a hook fastening.

Victoria & Albert Museum,
London (T.88 & A-1974)

Portrait of Madame Misia Sert by François Kollar, 1937

It was Misia who introduced Chanel to Parisian high society and artistic circles. Here she wears a star-spangled evening dress by Chanel.

While Chanel's day clothes retained their essential simplicity throughout the 1930s, her evening dresses and suits became more ornate and extravagant. Chanel had achieved her success through the simplicity of style she had learned earlier in the century and now, ironically, enjoyed her own forays into the revived frou-frou. She excelled in making long, diaphanous confections of fine muslins, silks, tulles, laces, ribbons, velvets and taffetas. Clearly inspired by the vogue for late 19th-century revivalism, Chanel created bare-shouldered and tiny-waisted crinolines and bustle dresses which often had veiled arms or were worn with shoulder-length lace fingerless gloves. The fullness of these dresses was achieved with padded fabric, rather than the horsehair petticoats or wire undergarments, which had supported 19th-century clothes.

Chanel's romantic dresses were complemented by floral accessories, such as white carnation headdresses which were worn with dramatic strapless black evening dresses

Illustration by René Bouet Willaumez in British *Vogue*, 21 September, 1938

The artist shows two striped velvet evening dresses by Chanel. The upswept hairstyles finished with coloured ribbon 'pinwheels' contribute to the romantic 'Victorian' revival style of these gowns.

The National Trust/Killerton House, Devon

Chanel's Tricolor evening dress, 1938-9

Red silk chiffon and grosgrain bodice fastening with tiny hooks and eyes with a red silk chiffon skirt. The edge of the bodice is trimmed with red, white and blue grosgrain ribbon, the colours of the Tricolor and featured in one of Chanel's last collections before the outbreak of war. It has the couture number 50031.

Victoria & Albert Museum, London (T.32-1978)

A Chanel gypsy dress, 1939

During the late 1930s Chanel's collections were imbued with romantic gypsy and peasant references. This photograph appeared in British *Vogue*, 22 February 1939.

Portrait of Chanel by François
Kollar, 1937

Chanel's full-length black lace
evening dress with veiled
sleeves was inspired by the
vogue for late 19th-century
revival styles during the mid to
late 1930s. She also wears a
camellia head-dress, a pearl
and coloured stone necklace, a
brooch on her waistband and
bracelets on each wrist.

or her favourite camellia or gardenia flowers made in fabric and pinned to the
shoulder or neckline. The dramatic use of black and white remained a popular
combination at Chanel. In spring 1938, her collection included both a full-length
chalk white crepe dress with a black satin sash and cotton lace bolero and a white
brocaded organza dress with its off-the-shoulder ruff finished with a huge black bow.

At the same time, Chanel's collections were again influenced by the styles,
colouring and fabrics of peasant and gypsy dress. Her full skirts were made in multi-
coloured taffetas, often striped and checked and worn with puff-sleeved, embroidered
and lace peasant-style blouses and short bolero jackets, with 'kerchiefs tied at the
neck. Even some of her usually restrained tailored day suits were decorated with
colourful pom-poms and decorative braids. In her autobiography, Diana Vreeland
recalls how Chanel loved peasant styles and, many years later, as Curator of Costume
at the Metropolitan Museum of Art (from 1972), she visited the Moscow Historical
Museum and saw the rich peasant dresses which had so influenced Chanel during the
late 1930s.

On 3 September 1939 Britain and France declared war on Germany following
Hitler's invasion of Poland. Three weeks later Chanel closed her House, stating that this
was no time for fashion, but continued to sell her perfume. In May 1940 the Germans
invaded France, reaching Paris in June. Many couturiers left Paris, while others decided
to remain open under German rule. Throughout the war Chanel lived at the Ritz
Hotel, which had been requisitioned by the Germans. When Paris was liberated in
1944 she went to live in Switzerland and did not return for another ten years.

Four COMEBACK 1953-1971

In her apartment above the rue Cambon showrooms Chanel adds the final touches to a suit modelled by Odile de Croy – only when jewellery was put on could she judge the total look of an outfit.

Conditions were inauspicious for fashion in the years following the conclusion of the Second World War. Indeed, the French press was on strike on 12 February 1947, the day that Christian Dior, formerly of the House of Lelong, revealed his New Look designs to the fashion world.

THE NEW LOOK

Dior had been set up in business by Boussac, the textile magnate. He introduced a radical change in fashion in the shape of long, full skirts, tight-fitting bodices and jackets with tiny waists which swept away the severe wartime boxy tops and short straight skirts. *Le Bar*, the first model in the collection, epitomised Dior's *Corolle* line. He was inspired to make skirts like the whorl of petals in an opening flower. He intended to dress women in the Belle Epoque revival style which had begun to appear before the outbreak of war. The collection was greeted by appreciative reviews.

Carmel Snow, editor-in-chief of the American magazine *Harper's Bazaar*, was the journalist who named the line the 'New Look'. Welcomed after the austerity of dress during the war the New Look, which revelled in luxury, represented hopes for a more prosperous and peaceful future. It gave a visible foretaste of the diminished role in society that women were expected to assume during the next decade. Dior was to reign as supreme leader of fashion for the next ten years.

The fashion world loved Dior's collections but shortages meant that it would be impossible for most women to emulate the look immediately, especially as some of the enormous skirts took as much as 20 yards of material. Sir Stafford Cripps, Britain's President of the Board of Trade, exclaimed at this extravagance 'There should be a law'. But despite the furore, Dior was unstoppable.

The return of glamour and femininity in dress also meant a new emphasis on foundation garments. Dior's magnificent dresses had a sub-structure of padding and stiffening, their waists were formed into the desired shape by tight 'waspie' corsets and bustle frills. Other designers, such as Jacques Fath, followed with lean, but equally restricting, lines. It was the complete antithesis of Chanel's philosophy of dress.

CHANEL RETURNS

By the time Chanel decided to begin work again in 1953, her achievements had passed into fashion history. Most of the Chanel premises on the rue Cambon had

Chanel photographed by
Robert Doisneau on the
mirrored staircase at 31 rue
Cambon, on the eve of her
comeback in 1954.

Opinion was divided when
Chanel re-opened her fashion
house. The critics found her
old-fashioned, but American
Vogue recognised the strength
of her tradition and her
hallmark; an easy casual look
in jersey and tweed was to
capture the American market.

This photograph was taken in Chanel's apartment above the rue Cambon.

A white crepe coat and dress. The coat is gently bloused over a tie-belt and trimmed with heavy bands of sable. *Vogue* showed a white crepe dress also trimmed with sable in September 1958. Both coat and dress are reminiscent of the grey silk jersey chemise designed in 1917. Chanel's own tweed suit with cardigan jacket typifies the look she evolved for herself which was widely copied. The emphasis is on relaxed elegance, comfort and luxury. Accessories include two-tone shoes.

been closed for 14 years and to a new generation her name represented no more than a label on a perfume bottle.

The post-war years were sad ones for Chanel. She made one of her brief visits to Paris in 1950 and was with Misia when she died on 15 October that year in the company of her closest friends. When they had left, Chanel washed and perfumed her friend's body and made up her face. She dressed her in white and put on her finest jewels and then laid her on a bed smothered in white flowers, with a single pink rose across her chest.

Her biographers have painted a picture of a bored, lonely, elderly woman and numerous stories have been told to explain her decision to work again at the age of 70. However, it seems most likely that the impetus came both from a desire to boost her flagging perfume sales and to oppose the new dictators of fashion. Interestingly, women had dominated the world of couture before the war with Chanel, Schiaparelli, Vionnet and Madame Grès all supreme. Now, in the 1950s, men imposed their views about how women should dress. Chanel was not impressed, remarking that 'Dressing women is not a man's job. They dress

Cocktail dress, 1958

This youthful dress has a bodice of navy and white striped silk finished with a large bow. The full skirt of white organdie is trimmed at the hem with the same striped silk is used for the bodice.

them badly because they scorn them.' (Galante, p.220)

During the summer of 1953, while she was still living in Lausanne, Pierre Wertheimer visited Chanel to express his concern that the sales of her perfume, Chanel No. 5, were falling in spite of Marilyn Monroe's much-quoted statement that she wore nothing but Chanel No. 5 in bed. He felt that a new Chanel perfume was not the answer. The market had grown strongly competitive and it was decided that the successful re-opening of her couture house would revive interest.

Chanel's return to couture was backed by the Wertheimers and Parfums Chanel, who financed 50 per cent of the collection, charging it to their publicity budget. Chanel's return created a flutter of interest in the fashion press. *Le Figaro, Elle, Paris-Match* and *France-Soir* published 'exclusive' interviews with her during November and December 1953. The *New York Herald Tribune* did the same in the States, while British *Vogue* retold her story the following February.

In these interviews Chanel outlined her reasons for returning to work. Sticking to her principles, she promised that she would once again make women look pretty and young, dismissed eccentricity in fashion and acclaimed comfort and function: 'A dress isn't right if it is uncomfortable. Nothings shows age more than the upper arms, cover them. Buttons must have buttonholes, pockets be in the right place, usable. A sleeve isn't right unless the arm lifts easily. Elegance in clothes means freedom to move freely.' (American *Vogue,* 15 February 1954).

Vogue stressed the point that Mademoiselle Chanel's looks and views were unchanged. In the pages of the magazine she announced that she would reach further than a handful of wealthy clients to dress thousands of women, and she was to fulfil her promise.

Preparations began in 1953, with Chanel returning only to 31 rue Cambon, refurbishing the boutique which had remained open for the sale of perfumes, the workrooms and her famous third-floor apartment. Now her days were spent in the rue Cambon, resting and entertaining in the apartment when she was not working, returning to her suite at the Ritz only to sleep.

Chanel produced 130 models for the collection which was awaited with eager anticipation, fuelled by the advance publicity. At last, on 5 February 1954 (a date chosen because 5 was Chanel's lucky number), the collection was revealed. Those who experienced the show at first hand found the atmosphere cold, silent and a little peculiar. Celia Bertin commented that Chanel was 'the prisoner of the period she influenced so strongly'. The great mirrors of the salon reflected a procession of mannequins with numbered cards, there was no music and none of the 'zip' that had come to be associated with the major fashion shows. Chanel stated firmly that she was offering couture, not theatre, but the old-fashioned style of presentation only served to underline the unfavourable reaction of the press. They thought her too old. As Chanel sat at the top of her mirrored staircase watching the mannequins parade, many journalists prepared their biting reviews.

In France, newspapers like *Le Figaro* and *France-Soir* wrote that her collection harked back to the 1920s and 1930s, that the world was not ready for a revival of these simple styles. In London the *Daily Express* headline spelt out 'A Fiasco'. On 18 February, the *Daily Herald's* Marge Proops summed up these reactions: 'How sad are these attempts to make a come-back. How very rarely they succeed... Once you're faded, it takes more than a name and memories of past triumphs to put you back in the spotlight.' Yet on 1 February Proops had commented on her dislike of Fath's 'whalebone straight jackets' and had found Dior's show disappointing. Two weeks later the *Daily Herald* carried the headline 'Who cares for comfort?' criticising corseted Paris fashions. Comments like these show that fashion writers were ready for a change. Unlike the European Press, the American magazine *Life* applauded Chanel's return in its issue of 1 March 1954. Eventually, others joined in.

Bettina Ballard, who was editor of French *Vogue*, describes the reaction of the press and buyers. The French press were almost unanimous in their dislike of the

White tweed suit,
1957 or 1958

The collarless jacket has four
pockets and is trimmed with a
navy and white braid. Both the
jacket and straight skirt are
top-stitched.

Detail of jacket lining.

The white silk lining is
stitched to the jacket which is
weighted with a gilt chain –
with flattened links – sewn
inside the hem. Chanel
continued to pay attention to
detail, to the *luxe caché*
(hidden luxury) firmly
associated with her garments.

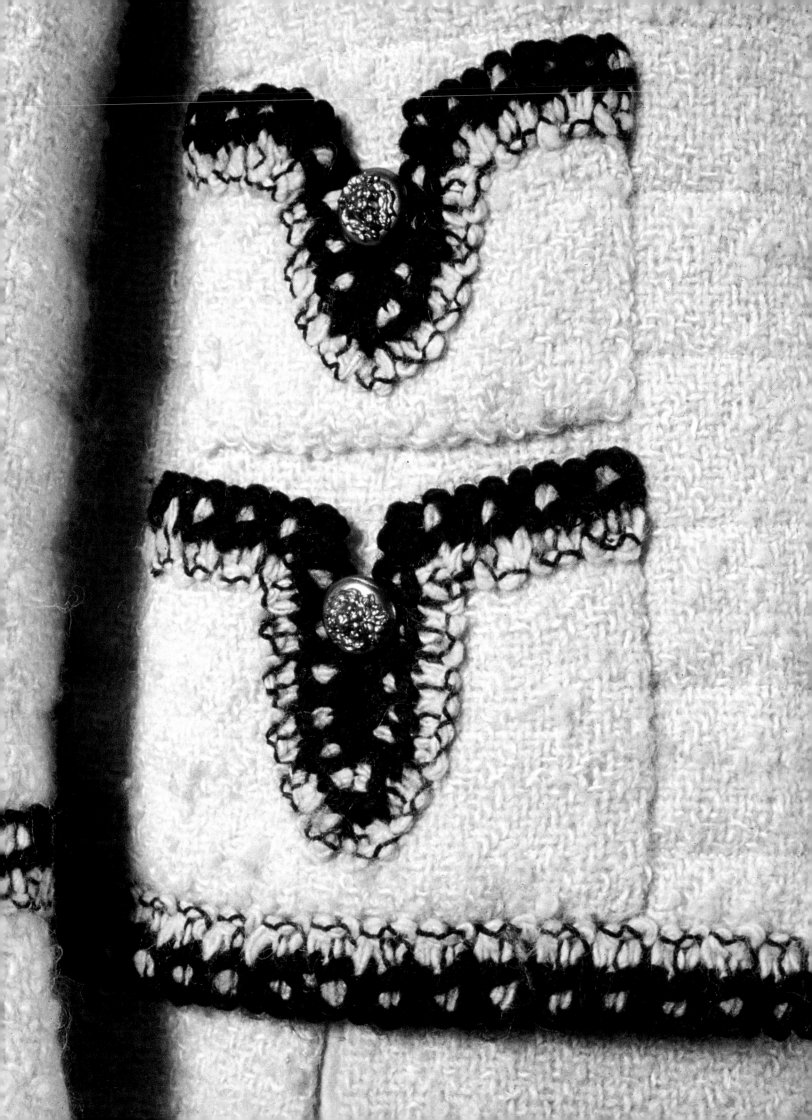

Detail of suit shown on
page 91

Vogue described a 'multiplicity
of pockets' as essential to
Chanel's suits, 'real pockets
made to hold a key, a lighter,
whatever...' here trimmed
with braid and fastened safely
with a gilt button.

Mannequin showing black
and white tweed suit from
Chanel's 1959 collection

Preparing for a show at the
House of Chanel, 1959

Mannequins posing in the rue Cambon boutique, mid 1950s

Chanel continued to use both black and white lace to great effect. These cocktail dresses may have been made from machine laces manufactured by the old established firm of Dognin, who supplied the House during the 1950s. The hair-bows and two-tone shoes are familiar accessories. Marie-Hélène Arnaud (seated) was a favourite House mannequin. A range of Chanel perfumes are just visible on the counter in the background

'This Year's suit', 1959

This photograph, taken outside the Chanel boutique in the rue Cambon, was reproduced in *Everywoman* Magazine in April, 1959. Of oatmeal coloured tweed, the textured surface contrasts strongly with the broad edgings of jersey. The blouse matches the jacket trimming. The suit is accessorised with a simple string of pearls, a flat, top-stitched hat, short white gloves and sling-back stilettos. Apart from the contemporary style of the hat and shoes, the outfit retains many elements of the Chanel look of the 1920s and 1930s. 'Chanel's philosophy has… permeated the fashion world' *Vogue* announced in the same month.

collection. Few customers bought and Ballard recalls that only about six outfits were sold. Ballard, however, had three pages of Chanel models photographed for *Vogue*, and these prefaced the March issue with Marie-Hélène Arnaud, Chanel's new mannequin, in a characteristic Chanel pose leaning against a wall with her hands in the pockets of the navy jersey suit with a gardenia on the lapel. Underneath the suit a white lawn blouse with a bow tie is buttoned on to the skirt at the waist, and crisp white cuffs are on display. A navy boater completes the outfit. Significantly, Ballard bought this model for herself. A cocktail dress in pink jersey with a wrap front and a draped skirt was also illustrated.

Vogue's reaction was divided. 'At its best, it has the easy, liveable look which is her great contribution to fashion history; at its worst it repeats the lines she made famous in the thirties: repeats rather than translates into contemporary terms.' However, *Vogue* also pointed out that styles were beginning to look back to the Chanel tradition and that other couturiers, led by Balenciaga, had shown variations on a looser line, an easy, bloused look. In fact, only Fath and Balmain remained faithful to a corseted fit.

Chanel, however, was undeterred by the adverse criticism. She blamed the

Black lace evening dress, late 1950s

This strapless sheath evening dress is constructed over a boned foundation, the trumpet-shaped skirt is supported by a layered petticoat heavily stiffened with a deep band of black net. Once worn by the top fashion model, Anne Gunning, Lady Nutting. Dresses similar to this one were featured in the magazines *Elle* and *Marie-Claire* in 1958. Cocktail and evening dresses of black or white lace or chiffon featured regularly in Chanel's collection during the 1950s and 1960s.

Victoria & Albert Museum, London (T.131-1990)

journalists: it was they who were wrong. She continued to work on, preparing her next collection with the support of Parfums Chanel, who by now were wary of the losses likely to be made. Parfums Chanel bought her out in May 1954, taking over the House. The Wertheimer brothers agreed that Chanel was to continue to receive royalties from perfume sales including No. 5, and the new men's scent 'Pour Monsieur'. Sole control of the collections was hers, and all the expenses were paid, including her apartment at the Ritz, secretaries and servants, telephone calls and even postage stamps.

The 1954 collections also included *mousseline* dresses and evening suits of gold-trimmed brocade or silver lamé. The Musée de la Mode et du Costume in Paris has a model gown from this year labelled 'Yvonne Atelier Paule No.46'; Chanel always numbered her models. Of white organdie, embroidered in red with an unusual design of tropical fish, this full-skirted dress has a stiffened tulle underskirt and a strapless boned bodice. It is youthful and contemporary with nothing of the 1930s about it. For day, Chanel used white tweed trimmed with red and navy, and also produced a brown suede coat made originally for her own use.

Detail of suit in Prince of
Wales tweed, 1959.

The black and white checked
surah silk edging the button,
pocket and cuff is also used for
the blouse and lining of this
suit, which was worn by
Hélène Lazareff, founder of
Elle magazine. The suit was
photographed by Henry
Clarke for *Vogue*, appearing in
the April 1959 issue

Between 1955 and 1957 Chanel remained faithful to a range of colours and
fabrics similar to those she had used before the war. Red, black, beige, white and blue
– especially navy – were all in evidence, with jersey, tweeds, satins, plain and printed
chiffons, brocades, velvets and lamés occasionally rubbing shoulders with some of the
new man-made fibres. She used black nylon, for example, for a cocktail dress in the
mid-1950s. In 1955, Chanel's designs included a belted tunic dress in red jersey for
day and a full-skirted gold brocade dress with matching jacket for evening. Her
preoccupation with the fit of sleeves is evident in this jacket which survives in the
collection of the Fashion Institute of Technology, New York. The material has been
cut into horizontal bands sewn together to follow the shape of the arm. In 1955
Chanel created the first of the quilted leather handbags which were to become
classics in their own right. The bags were available in soft leather or jersey in shades
of navy, beige, brown or black. The fabric was stitched over padding to give the
quilted effect, and bags were finished with a shoulder strap of leather plaited with gilt
chain similar to those used in the linings of her suits.

The next collection enjoyed more success, and by 1957 Chanel was back on top
again. Some of the best-dressed women in the world were to be numbered among
her clients, including Diana Vreeland, Grace Kelly, Lauren Bacall, Ingrid Bergman,
Elizabeth Taylor and Marlene Dietrich, whom she had dressed in the 1930s and who
also had only recently returned to the stage.

In 1957 Dior died of a heart attack, leaving Chanel once more the undisputed
leader of fashion. In this year she won the Neiman-Marcus award for fashion and *Elle*
put Chanel and Texas-born House model Suzy Parker on their cover.

Chanel had been constantly refining her style to reach this point. Although she
would state vehemently that she never did the same thing twice, her collections, and
particularly the suits, did in fact repeat a formula, changing only fabrics and details
like buttons. In September 1957, British *Vogue* published a drawing by Bouché of
the year's Chanel suit. In this season she reintroduced a skirt with a side pleat and a
jacket with gilt buttons. Keeping to the same colour ranges, Chanel added braid to
the jackets of her suits.

In 1958 *Vogue* thought Chanel 'more truly of today' than many designers half her
age. Chanel had kept her promise; her style was much copied, from the jersey suits to
gold chains and pearls, sailor hats and sling-back shoes with contrasting toe caps.
Women copied her models' hair-styles, wearing a straight-cut fringe, fluffing out their
hair at the sides, securing it with a ribbon bow at the back.

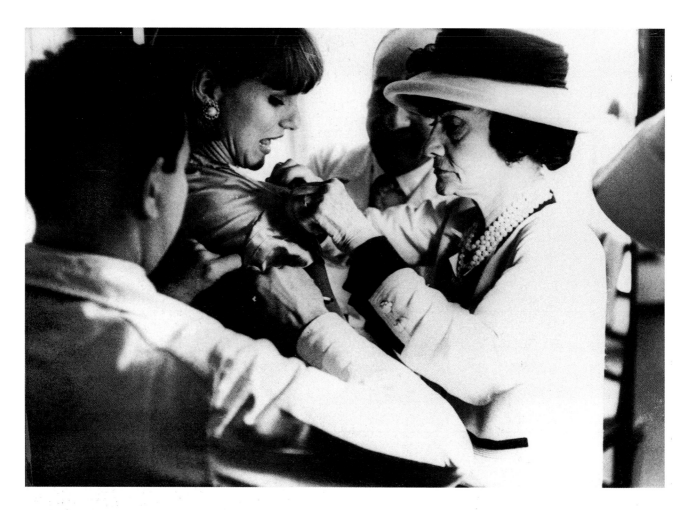

Sante Forlano's photographs of Marie-Hélène Arnaud illustrated the style for *Vogue*'s September 1958 issue. For day, they showed a cardigan suit in large black and white checked tweed fabric over a sleeveless blouse of black jersey, with jewel-like buttons securing the jacket cuffs. The skirt was straight, the look completed by a tweed pillbox hat worn at the back of the head, and a gold chain necklace. For evening, the magazine chose a cardigan suit, neat and simple, but made in black velvet with a blouse in the same white satin material as the lining. The small brimmed velvet hat had a single jewelled pin and short strands of chain and pearls ornamented the necklace.

There is something familiar about these pieces, especially the white crepe tunic dress with a band of sable at the hem. Gently bloused into a tie-belt, with a tubular skirt, this dress was reminiscent of Chanel's gowns of 1917, yet at the same time was entirely of the 1950s. It is a good example of how the Chanel style offered a secure, timeless alternative to the ever-changing lines of fashion.

An extremely successful suit of 1959 was modelled by the Comtesse Guy d'Arcangues for *Vogue* in April 1959. Examples of this model survive in the collections of the Union Français des Arts et du Costume, Paris, and in the Design Laboratory of the Fashion Institute of Technology, New York (the latter was worn by the American actress Lauren Bacall). In black and white Prince of Wales check silk, the suit was lined and faced with the same grey, black and white broad-checked silk as the blouse. Perfection lay in the details: two buttons at the waist, to secure the blouse to the skirt and prevent gaps or wrinkling, and a flat gilt chain sewn to the lining of the jacket to weight it. These details are unseen but add to the luxury and success of the final garment.

In the same collection, Chanel showed black for evening – her 'perfect' suit of black broadcloth with white silk lining and blouse, and also a black lace dress with a full flared skirt, ribbon belt and tiny ribbon straps, repeating a success of the 1930s

Chanel photographed by Douglas Kirkland backstage at the showing of her collection in 1962. Her mannequins endured hours of standing while Mademoiselle rearranged and pinned garments.

Photograph by Douglas Kirkland backstage at the Chanel show, 1962. Chanel explains the adjustment of a hemline to the managers of her atelier. She wore her scissors on a ribbon around her neck, so that they were to hand when needed.

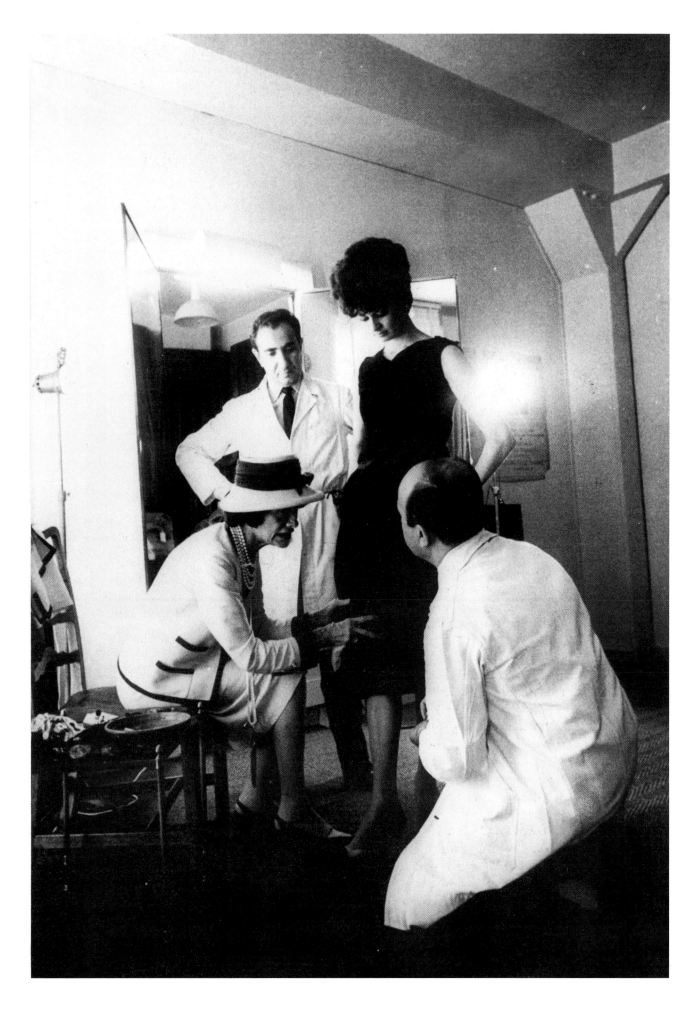

Brooch in Renaissance style made of gilt metal set with *faux* gemstones and artificial pearls, with a large pendant pearl

'Women can wear fortunes that cost nothing', said Chanel of her costume jewellery. In 1978, Christie's London sale of Chanel's personal collection attracted prices which might have been expected of real gemstones. A glass and gilt brooch sold for £1,600.

Pearl necklace, earrings and a brooch in the form of a cross with *faux* gemstones in a gilt mount, 1960-65

Carefully placed costume jewellery remained an essential part of the Chanel style. Gilt chains, artificial pearls and brooches composed of multi-coloured glass stones in gilt settings were often inspired by historical and religious forms, such as the Cross. Such pieces had become firmly associated with the House of Chanel and were widely copied.

when Chanel had been well known for her lace evening dresses. Princesse Odile de Croy was photographed wearing a nubbly, beige wool, straight cardigan coat, piped and lined with navy blue silk, with a loosely tied scarf at the neck – another element carried through from the first decades of the 20th century.

JEWELLERY

Chanel thought a suit 'naked' without jewellery. Her return to prominence in the 1950s encouraged the reappearance of costume jewellery in high fashion. Layers of gilt chains, glass stones and pearls once again became associated with the House of Chanel. Robert Goossens began working for Chanel in 1954. He produced works in gilt and pearl for her. He had previously worked as a goldsmith and saw himself as a craftsman and interpreter rather than a creator, working closely with Chanel on themes for the collection. Chanel was known to restyle his prototype necklaces and turn them into belts.

By the mid-1950s costume jewellery was much in demand once more. Mme Gripoix, whose firm had supplied Chanel before the war, started to work for her again, producing ornate styles that were inspired by the Renaissance and that were widely copied.

Woollen tweed bouclé coat with silk trimming and lining, 1960s. Worn by Lady Nutting.

A winter-weight wool is lined with a summer-weight silk in shocking pink. This coat recalls the wool and chiffon models Chanel made in the 1930s using a heavy woven wool or wool jersey lined with delicate floral printed chiffon to match a chiffon dress. There is an example in the collections of the Costume Institute, New York. Here, the bouclé wool buttons are edged with pink silk, and the collar is faced with the same silk. The lining is quilted in vertical lines adding substance and warmth, and creating a decorative finish.

Victoria & Albert Museum, London (T.128-1990)

CHANEL COPIES

Before the launch of her 'comeback' collection Chanel wrote to Carmel Snow, editor-in-chief of *Harper's Bazaar*: 'The current climate in Paris in which more and more women are shown collections they cannot afford is pushing me to do something completely different. One of my primary goals is to have an American manufacturer produce a ready-to-wear line on a royalty basis. I feel that this would arouse considerable interest throughout the world'. (Quoted in Madsen, p.284).

Chanel believed that her style would be affirmed by high-street copies – after all, copying is the sincerest form of flattery. She also realised that cheaper versions of her clothes could never truly imitate the cut and luxury of the originals.

In the 1950s women were no longer ordering dresses by the dozen from the couture houses, who protected and partly financed their collections by releasing patterns, photographs and toiles of their designs in exchange for a fee from manufacturers. The *Chambre Syndicale de la Couture Parisienne* existed to prevent the pirating of designs which were registered with them. They embargoed the release

Violet and navy wool
suit, c.1963

Irregular-textured violet wool
jacket and skirt. The short
double-breasted jacket has
three-quarter-length sleeves
edged with navy taffeta and
trimmed with gold buttons.
The collar is faced with navy
taffeta and the skirt is lined
with the same material. This is
said to be the model made in
pink for Jackie Kennedy which
she was wearing on the day of
the assassination of the
President in Dallas in 1963.

of photographs to the press until after the shows. Consequently, journalists rushed to
communicate the latest designs and details seen at the Paris shows to the public.

The fashion journalist Ernestine Carter remembered that you could not make a
squiggle in your notebook without running the risk of having it confiscated. Yet it
was difficult to stop the more unscrupulous reporters from passing on sketches.
Chanel paid no heed to the regulations, making the trade situation work to her
advantage. She permitted her collections to be photographed by the press. Cecil
Beaton expressed his surprise at being allowed to photograph her at work on her
models for her 1954 collections.

Times had changed and the demand for upmarket ready-to-wear and versions of
high-fashion style made for the cheaper end of the market were to bolster couture in
the years ahead. Givenchy and Balenciaga followed suit and the *Chambre* dropped
the press embargo. It is often said that Chanel's saviours in the 1950s were the
American mass-market manufacturers of New York's Seventh Avenue, who eagerly
bought her designs to supply an enthusiastic American audience for whom Chanel's
casual elegance was just right.

Details of the lilac mohair suit

Left: Sleeve detail showing gilt buttons fastening the blouse cuff and jacket. The buttons of Chanel suits are always functional as well as decorative.

Right: Close-up of the Iris print lining the jacket. The parallel lines of stitching keeps the lining in place and quilts the garment in a decorative manner.

Lilac mohair wool suit with blouse printed with a design of flag irises in mauves and browns on a cream ground. The skirt and jacket are lined with the same patterned material and the loosely-woven mohair is overstitched in vertical lines. The jacket is finished with gilt filigree buttons. This lightweight suit from the Spring 1964 collection was worn by Baroness Alain de Rothschild.

Victoria & Albert Museum, London (T.90 & A-1990)

In the 1950s and 1960s Paris still influenced retailers. The British chain-store Wallis specialised in Chanel copies and their popularity may have played a part in reintroducing the style to British women. From the late 1950s Wallis bought so many toiles that they were offered concessionary prices. *Vogue* showed the designs brought back to England in 1964 by Jeffrey Wallis: 'They proved Britain's fashion industry can work in top gear, bring Paris in fast'. In Britain, Jaeger and Marks and Spencer were also selling ready-to-wear versions of suits to different market sectors by the 1960s, and in the United States the department store Saks on Fifth Avenue did the same.

1960 TO 1971

The versatile Chanel suit appealed to many women seeking functional and elegant clothes. By the early 1960s it was regarded as a classic, the sort of thing to wear for luncheons or to the office. However, women were also advised that matching the blouse to the lining of the jacket was not always a practical idea as the blouse naturally wore out much more quickly than the suit, which never looked as good with any other blouse.

The decade of the 1960s is much celebrated as the era of youth, and of new attitudes as well as of new technology and materials, and this was reflected by the progressive Paris designers such as André Courrèges and Paco Rabanne. Against this background it might seem that there was no longer room for tradition, but Mademoiselle Chanel continued to provide just that, by always subtly reworking the same styles. She abhorred the miniskirt, saying that knees were unsightly and that the fashion was immodest, in spite of the fact that she had herself introduced what were considered radically short skirts in the 1920s.

The British press saw her as a specialist in the art of dress for the not-so-young. An article in the *Evening News* on 14 February 1960 lists her recommendations for

Black worsted crepe jacket and dress with black silk stockinette hat, mid 1960s.

This model, no. 37750, was purchased from Christie's sale of Chanel's personal collection. The look is severe and school girlish. The pristine white collar and cuffs were themes carried through from the suit which launched Chanel's return to couture in 1954. Here the garments are neat and functional without decoration, although the dress is lined throughout with black silk. Similar dresses with hip-length jackets were interpreted in rich materials such as brocades and patterned velvets for evening wear in 1966.

Victoria & Albert Museum, London (T.22c-1979, T.37-1983)

perfectly cut, simple clothes such as tailored dresses, 'not because they are my speciality, but because they still dress a woman of over 40 to her best', and interestingly the article continues, 'Don't wear black... Black is OK for a woman of 55, not for a woman of 40'.

Chanel's clothes were to make a reappearance in the cinema. In 1961 she was invited to dress Romy Schneider for the episode *Work* in Chanel's old friend Luchino Visconti's film, *Boccaccio 70*. Chanel also designed for Delphine Seyrig in Alain Resnais' film of the same year, *Last Year at Marienbad*.

During the 1960s Chanel became a favourite of Jacqueline Kennedy, although she had once called America's First Lady 'the worst dressed woman on any continent'. Jackie Kennedy was also dressed by Oleg Cassini, who claimed that he aimed for a 'true personal inspiration' like that of Chanel.

Chanel continued to pay attention to the unseen details: fine linings would sometimes be stitched down in parallel lines resembling quilting, and this might even be continued through to the skirts; jackets were always equipped with the flat gilt chain to help them to hang properly.

Detail of dark red bouclé wool suit with navy wool jersey trim, and matching jersey top, 1960s

The jacket has the collar and cuffs faced with navy wool jersey which also trims the jacket pockets and buttons on the jacket and skirt. The skirt has four gently flared panels for fit and comfort. The short-sleeved top of navy wool jersey has a perky bow at the neck. This suit was worn by Lady Nutting. As Anne Gunning she was a celebrated fashion model of the 1950s.

Victoria & Albert Museum, London (T.123 to B-1990)

A Chanel suit of 1965

By the early 1960s the distinctive cardigan suit was well established, and was to be interpreted in a variety of materials for day and evening wear throughout the decade. The staple materials were jersey supplied by the firms of Lesur and Gerondeau, and Linton tweeds from Carlisle, northern England a firm which had first provided Chanel with tweeds in 1928. This suit in shades of green, orange, brown and beige tweed has a stand-up collar and pleated skirt. The edges of the jacket are trimmed with a green wool to tone with the tweed. The gilt buttons bear a lion's head motif based on Chanel's astrological sign, Leo.

Katharine Hepburn in the title
role of *Coco*, photographed by
Cecil Beaton in 1969

Beaton designed 250 stylised
versions of Chanel clothes for the
Broadway musical, including this
suit based on Chanel's 1965
collection. The ingenious set
design solved the problem of
quick scene changes from
showroom to apartment by
placing the mirrored staircase
and beige carpet of 31 rue
Cambon on a revolving stage.

Quilted leather handbag with
twisted leather and gilt chain
shoulder strap, c.1963

The first bag of this type
appeared in 1955. Originally
made in a choice of two
materials, leather or jersey, it
was available in a range of
typical 'Chanel' colours –
beige, navy, brown or black
lined with red grosgrain or
leather. The bags are still
craftsman-made with hand-
stitched quilting, and with the
plaited shoulder strap have
become a classic accessory. The
linked 'C' logo on the gilt clasp
is a more recent addition.

In 1960 Chanel made coarse, white tweed cardigan suits edged with navy and scarlet braid. Throughout the decade she made suits in pastel multicoloured tweeds as well as the classic beige and white. For evening they were interpreted in gold lamé brocade or fabrics such as chenille with a lurex thread. Chanel's choice of fabrics varied from soft green and orange Scottish tweeds in the early 1960s to pinks, from the palest through to strong raspberries woven with blues and yellows or with greens and white towards the end of the decade. These suits were usually trimmed with gilt buttons, sometimes bearing the linked 'C' insignia.

In 1963 Chanel brought back smart navy and white in a navy jersey blazer jacket over a tucked white shirt, and in 1964 introduced glittering gold trouser suits for evening and navy 'sailor pants' for day. Evening dresses were wisps of black chiffon or glamorous tubes of white sequins. In 1966 a suit of white cloqué – a blistered silk fabric – was shown with a wrapped skirt and silk jersey blouse and proved that she could adapt her style to the short-skirted 1960s.

COCO

Chanel was indeed a legend in her own lifetime, perhaps a legend twice over. In 1969, with Chanel's agreement, Katharine Hepburn played the great Mademoiselle in the Alan Jay Lerner Broadway musical production, *Coco*, which concentrated on Chanel's story from the time of her comeback in 1953-4. One of the most expensive musicals in Broadway history, *Coco* opened on 18 December 1969. Cecil Beaton designed the costumes and the show received much media attention.

Beaton's drawings were as much a caricature of her work as designs for the stage. He later said, 'I knew people would criticise me for designing Chanel clothes, but if we had put authentic Chanel dresses on stage they would have looked like they came from the thrift shop'. (Spencer, p.58). Beaton's designs were a triumph and in 1970 he received a Tony award for them.

On 24 December 1970 Chanel launched a new perfume. It was called No. 19, after her birthday, and also to make clear that it was intended to appeal to a younger age group. The perfume as a success and has remained so to the present day.

The last years of Chanel's life were solitary ones. It has sometimes been said that work was all she had. Her younger sister, Antoinette had died long ago, and her aunt Adrienne had died in 1955, five years after Misia.

Chanel's legendary maxims, her bitterness and cruel remarks have been repeated many times by her biographers. She was often extremely rude about the couturiers who respected and admired her talents, such as Dior, Yves Saint Laurent and Balenciaga (although the latter said she didn't know how to cut!), yet the American designer Norman Norell paid homage to her with a collection 'in the manner of Chanel'.

Gabrielle Chanel continued to work right up until the time of her death on 10 January 1971 in her austere bedroom at the Ritz. The memorial service held at the Madeleine was attended by many of the designers she had attacked, as well as friends such as Salvador Dali and the dancer and choreographer Serge Lifar, clients and mannequins. She was buried in Lausanne, beneath a tomb carved with the lion heads of her birth sign, Leo.

Cecil Beaton subsequently wrote (Buckle, 1979, p.412) that in his view 'Chanel had qualities and talents that are very rare, she was a genius, and all her faults must be forgiven for that reason'.

Five   THE HOUSE OF CHANEL TODAY

Chanel, ready-to-wear for
Spring/Summer 1994
photographed by
Karl Lagerfeld

Various sources have inspired
this outfit: inspiration has
bubbled up from Ragga for
the bra top, from B-boy for
the baggy trousers and braces
and traditional Chanel designs
have been recalled for the two-
tone shoes, cardigan jacket
and the camellias worn in
the hair.

For the 12 years following the founder's death the House of Chanel was at an all-time low. Lacking progressive direction it became indelibly associated with an ageing, well-to-do clientèle who continued to purchase classics designed in the Chanel tradition by Gaston Berthelot (working for the House from 1971 to 1973), who had formerly worked for the House of Dior in New York. In the early 1970s attempts were made to project a younger and more exciting image by the promotion as the face of Chanel of the French film star, Catherine Deneuve. She was to promote No.5 perfume sales in the United States. having been voted 'most beautiful woman in the world' by *Look* magazine in 1968. When Alain Wertheimer took the helm in 1974, the company focused upon expanding into the lucrative American youth market, and selected Cheryl Tiegs to promote its No.5 perfume.

With international couture sales still on the wane in 1978 a ready-to-wear line was introduced by Philippe Guibourgé, who had designed with Jacques Fath and Christian Dior. An ambitious programme was started and just one year later there were Chanel boutiques throughout the United States, Canada and Europe as well as one situated on the ground floor of Chanel's rue Cambon premises. From 1974 haute couture at Chanel was designed by Jean Cazaubon and Yvonne Dudel and from 1980 Ramone Esparza joined the team. However, it was not until 1983, when Karl Lagerfeld was invited to design the boutique and accessories collections for the still-ailing fashion house, that the name of Chanel once again became top international fashion news.

KARL LAGERFELD DESIGNS FOR CHANEL

Karl Lagerfeld, son of a wealthy Swedish father, was brought up in Hamburg where, during his early years, he developed a passion for beautiful clothes. In 1952, when he was 14, he went to Paris to study art. Two years later he entered a competition sponsored by the International Wool Secretariat with a design for a coat, which earned him joint first prize. (His fellow winner was Yves Saint Laurent who had designed a dress). Pierre Balmain was one of the judges and subsequently employed Lagerfeld and it was at Balmain that he was to learn the skills of haute couture. In 1958 he became head designer at Patou.

From 1964 he acted as a freelance designer for the fashion houses of Chloë, Krizia, Cadette and Max Mara and also worked for the shoe manufacturer Charles Jourdan.

Karl Lagerfeld (front, second left) after his first couture show for Chanel, 1983.

Ines de le Fressange modelling haute couture for Spring/Summer 1985.

The timeless appeal of Chanel. Here, Ines de la Fressange models ready-to-wear blazer, baggy trousers and two-tone shoes. These clothes are as desirable today as in the 1920s and 1930s.

Since 1965 Lagerfeld has designed for the progressive Italian fur company Fendi. He was employed by Chanel from 1983 and, from 1984, additionally started his own label. In 1992 he returned as head designer to the House of Chloë. Karl Lagerfeld is a prolific designer, producing 16 collections a year while most couturiers design two. That he is also highly talented can be seen in the way that, season after season, he creates successful collections with a distinct character for each of the various Houses he designs for.

Karl Lagerfeld showed his first haute couture collection under the name of Chanel in January 1983. From the outset he incorporated Chanel's signature designs into his work, initially fairly literally and later with greater irreverence. He created his own archive by cutting out every reference to Chanel from his vast collection of magazines and used them to compile scrapbooks of Chanel's work into which he dips to the present day.

Lagerfeld's designs made their début on the Chanel catwalk with lavish, black evening dresses which were beaded and embroidered with motifs taken from Chanel's beloved Coromandel screens which decorated her apartment. The cut of his dresses combined her revolutionary 1920s dropped-waist Garçonne style with her more body-moulding evening silhouettes of the 1930s. Some of Lagerfeld's garments were fish-tailed and others had diamanté jewellery inspired by Chanel and Iribe's 1932 Bijoux des Diamants designs.

Lagerfeld has continued to exploit the Chanel look to the present day, sometimes paying homage to her classic styles and at other times parodying them mercilessly. He never promised to be reverential to the Chanel label and has rightly claimed that the revived success of the House lies in his departure from Chanel's strict dicta. In her own day Chanel was an iconoclast and he has said that it is the youthful, ground-breaking aspects of her career which most excite him. He also states that, in his view, Chanel was indeed a highly-talented designer but was also a great self-publicist. This,

Kirát (right) and Diane de Witt (left) model lavishly embroidered and beaded haute couture evening dresses, for Autumn/Winter 1983-4.

Group of Chanel models wearing classic Chanel-style suits in pastel colours embellished with masses of costume jewellery for Spring/Summer 1990.

he asserts, has assured her a legendary place in fashion history, a place that the many biographies and books such as this undoubtedly perpetuate.

Chanel's appropriation of clothing traditionally worn by men was considered radical in the 1920s. To have looked to the dress of the working man for stylistic inspiration for the world's most wealthy women was even more so. Today, Lagerfeld looks not to the utilitarian dress of the working man, but to the styles of the many sub-cultures seen on the streets of London and New York for some of his ideas.

Chanel herself always stated that the success of her style could not be measured by its influence on the catwalk, but by its proliferation on the streets and today this is a two-way process. Among the most tangible examples of this bubble-up process are Lagerfeld's B-boy bum-bags produced for Autumn/Winter 1989 and his leather biker style clothes, for Autumn/Winter 1992-3, which incorporated Chanel's classic chains and quilting. His biker boots in black leather, laced from top to bottom, and trimmed with the Chanel initials in gold metal, were such a success that boutiques around the world quickly sold out and had to create waiting lists for these luxury fashion items. Fetishistic dress has inspired his leather corsets and garments adorned with bondage straps and, in complete contrast, he has teamed sporty training shoes with Chanel's classic suits. For the Spring/Summer 1994 collections Black Ragga and B-boy styles have clearly inspired his work.

Some of this inspiration is imbued at first hand; Lagerfeld is friends, for example, with the Afrocentric rap band Arrested Development. Secondary sources must include films, television and magazines. Whatever the case, the references he extracts are purely stylistic and lose their sub-cultural and ideological significance when applied to high fashion. In the 1990s fashion is pluralistic and both Chanel's haute couture and ready-to-wear catwalks clearly reflect this stylistic diversity.

As always, it is the most radical part of any designer's output which creates press pictures and copy. It is often the way that Chanel's clothes are styled by, for example,

Supermodel Claudia Schiffer in a black evening dress with a jewelled chainmail front inspired by Chanel's 1930s jewellery designs. Haute couture for Autumn/Winter 1990-1.

Top-selling leather biker inspired outfit. Ready-to-wear for Autumn/Winter 1992-3.

Karl Lagerfeld photographed the supermodels Christy Turlington and Linda Evangelista wearing sequined surf-style jackets with stretchy lycra leggings for his Spring/Summer 1991 collections.

Ready-to-wear for Autumn/Winter 1990-1

Karl Lagerfeld adds quilted leather sleeves to this bright pink and black wool mini-skirted suit with leather trim. In the manner of the Surrealists, who were fascinated by displacement, the model wears a hat in the form of Chanel's classic quilted leather bag.

combining a supremely elegant jacket with a micro mini, exceptionally high heels and a bizarre hat, which can give the impression that they are unwearable. However, Chanel's clients appreciate the theatricality of the shows and often order the jackets seen there, but with longer skirts and more conservative accessories. Ultimately, Lagerfeld has succeeded in enticing to the House of Chanel a youthful clientèle who want to be at fashion's cutting edge while at the same time retaining the loyalty of the more traditional *aficionados* by producing for them understated, elegant designs.

Like Chanel, Lagerfeld has the practical skills so necessary for the making of luxury clothing. Indeed, his traditional couture training was a rare skill among top designers of the 1980s. While Chanel worked with fabric directly onto the body,

The more outrageous face of Karl Lagerfeld for Chanel.

Black lace evening wear inspired by Ragga and worn with face covering caged, black feather hat by Philip Treacy for Chanel. Haute couture for Spring/Summer 1994.

Claudia Schiffer modelling youthful ready-to-wear sportswear for Autumn/Winter 1993-4.

Underwear as outerwear at the Chanel show, Spring/Summer 1993

Here Karl Lagerfeld decorates his white cotton vest and knickers with a black fabric camellia and teams them with a classic tweed jacket, signature bag chain slung around the waist and monochrome glasses with the Chanel insignia.

Lagerfeld has always preferred to sketch his ideas. These seemingly simple line sketches are, in fact, accurate working drawings in which every line has significance and can be read with ease by Chanel's highly skilled head dressmaker and tailor. By carefully following these drawings they make a toile in calico and then Karl Lagerfeld will make any necessary amendments before the sample is made-up in luxurious fabrics.

The House of Chanel no longer owns textile factories but instead commissions small, specialist manufacturers such as Linton Tweeds of Carlisle, northern England, to produce exclusive fabrics. Unusual tweeds remain top sellers, and each season new textiles are developed. Karl Lagerfeld designs five collections for Chanel each year; two ready-to-wear, two haute couture and one cruise collection.

THE CHANEL WORKSHOPS TODAY

Haute couture clothing production at Chanel is divided between the tailoring and dressmaking workshops, which are situated above the couture salon and ready-to-wear

Haute couture evening wear
with Classical inspiration
modelled by Linda Evangelista
for Spring/Summer 1994.

Bra top and shorts with
matching jacket and hat in
Chanel's classic tweed fabric.
Ready-to-wear for
Spring/Summer 1994.

Navy blue ready-to-wear suit for Spring/Summer 1994.

Classic nautical designs such as this reefer jacket and striped top remain top sellers at Chanel. The famous House name and logo are proudly displayed. Photograph by Karl Lagerfeld

Chanel suit for Spring/Summer 1994

A modern variation on a classic theme. This monochrome ensemble consists of striped body and white cotton suit, of jacket and hipster mini skirt, with black plastic braid trim. It is accessorised with the signature Chanel chain and a spiky plastic hat. Photograph by Karl Lagerfeld

boutiques in the rue Cambon. M Paquito is head of the *atelier tailleur*, the haute couture tailoring workshop, and Mme Christiane heads the *atelier flou*, the dressmaking workshop. Together they are responsible for producing the designs at every stage, supervising the work schedules, production, fabrics and other supplies. They each have a team of between 35 and 40 workers, which often expands by another 10 or so just before the shows when work schedules accelerate.

The rigid hierarchy of the workforce has remained unchanged since the foundation of Chanel's fashion empire. The apprentices, who form the bottom of the pyramid, receive training in-house and some attend specialist college courses for one or two days each week. Once qualified, the apprentice may be promoted to *seconde main débutante*, then *seconde main qualifiée*, *première main débutante*, *seconde* and finally *premier d'atelier*.

Claudia Schiffer wears a youthful variation on the classic Chanel suit. Haute couture for Spring/Summer 1994.

The *premier* is the person who conducts fittings, together with the head of Haute Couture, either M Paquito or Mme Christiane as appropriate. There are at least two personal fittings for each couture garment made. The House of Chanel recognises that the busy lives of many of its clients prevent them from travelling to Paris and it is not unusual for M Pacquito or Mme Christiane to fly to America or elsewhere for fittings. Special shows of clothes will be staged for good clients and luxurious, glossy brochures, often with photographs by Karl Lagerfeld, also act as ambassadors for Chanel's collections abroad.

All haute couture clothing is made in the rue Cambon. The skills of couture are very much alive and there remains a small, discerning and very wealthy clientèle who appreciates, and is prepared to pay for, the luxury of haute couture clothing. For example, there have been many orders placed for the black or white pleated silk

Linda Evangelista models printed stretch sportwear with an abundance of jewellery and a pastel variation on the classic Chanel bag. Spring/Summer 1991. Photograph by Karl Lagerfeld.

blouses that were shown for Spring/Summer 1994. Hand pleating the fabric alone takes 200 hours. Lace is applied to each pleat and then the blouse is made up. Much of the stitching for haute couture clothing is carried out by hand. On the whole, one person makes one garment throughout, although the trainees may perform some of the more routine tasks. Beading and embroidery is sent out to the house of Lesage which works to Karl Lagerfeld's designs. Although sales of haute couture clothing are rising in 1994, it remains a loss-making industry.

THE CHANEL BUSINESS

In the mid 1980s when the economic boom was at its peak, the top Paris houses also enjoyed greater success with sales up between 25 and 30 per cent. Much of this increased business was provided by American clients and created an increasingly important Middle Eastern market. However, by 1987 this market had declined dramatically as the worldwide recession bit and it took several years to show any revival.

Today there are just 2000 to 3000 clients for haute couture clothing worldwide. Of these, the House of Chanel has around 150 ordering from each haute couture collection. Nowadays, it is ready-to-wear that forms the mainstay of clothing sales. Since the late 1980s Chanel's business has been equally divided between Europe, the United States and Asia. The Japanese in particular are great devotees of the Chanel label. Throughout Europe there are some 36 Chanel retail outlets, 52 in the United States and 20 in Japan while Australia, Canada, Hong Kong, Singapore, Taiwan and Korea also boast Chanel ready-to-wear shops.

The historic links between the fashion house and Parfums Chanel means that Chanel is one of the very few fashion houses to have its own perfume factory instead of commissioning perfumes from other companies. Furthermore Chanel refuses to sell its name to any licensee, but rather it insists on sole control of all products that bear its luxurious and internationally-respected lable. No.5 is the top-selling perfume in Britain and France and ranks among the top five in America and Germany. Overall, it is the world's top-selling perfume, with sales of some ten million bottles a year. The range of perfumes has also been expanded since Chanel's death to include Cristalle (1974), Antaeus pour Homme (1981), Coco (1984), No.5 Eau de Parfum (1986) and Egoiste for men (1990). Jacques Helleu is Chanel's artistic director for perfumes and cosmetics.

The House of Chanel continues to be owned by the Wertheimer family and is the only one of the large couture houses to remain in private hands. Once again, Chanel is expanding along the rue Cambon; numbers 27, 29 and 31 house the ready-to-wear boutique and, as always, the haute couture salon is situated on the first floor at 31. The watch and jewellery boutique, opened in 1990, is just around the corner in Place Vendôme. In 1993 Chanel re-launched a range of precious jewellery, taking many of the designs from Chanel's 1932 Bijoux de Diamants exhibition (see page 69).

The House of Chanel today recognises that commercial success ultimately lies in re-working Chanel's signature designs in a modern idiom. That the essence of these designs remains so desirable is due to Karl Lagerfeld's successful interpretation and is ultimately an accolade to the founder – Gabrielle Chanel.

Selected Bibliography

Baillen, Claude *Chanel Solitaire*, Editions Gallimard, Paris, 1971

Beaton, Cecil *The Glass of Fashion*, Weidenfeld & Nicholson, London, 1954

Buckle, Richard, ed., *Cecil Beaton Self-Portrait with Friends The Selected Diaries of Cecil Beaton 1926-1974*, Weidenfeld & Nicolson, London, 1979

Buckle, Richard, ed. *Dancing for Diaghilev*, John Murray, London, 1960

Charles Roux, Edmonde *Chanel and Her World*, Weidenfeld & Nicolson, London, 1981

Charles Roux, Edmonde *L'Irregulière*, Grasset, Paris, 1974

Coleridge, Nicholas *The Fashion Conspiracy*, Heinemann, London, 1988

Evans, Caroline and Thornton, Minna *Women and Fashion: A New Look*, Quartet Books, London, 1989

Field, Leslie *Bendor, The Golden Duke of Westminster*, Weidenfeld & Nicolson, London, 1983

Galante, Pierre *Mademoiselle Chanel*, Henry Regnery Company, Chicago, 1973

Gold, Arthur and Fizdale, Robert *Misia*, Alfred A. Knopf, New York, 1980

Haedrich, Marcel *Coco Chanel, Her Life, Her Secrets*, Little, Brown & Co, New York, 1971

Hawes, Elizabeth *Fashion is Spinach*, Random House, New York, 1938

Hein, Janine *Paris Haute Couture*, Panorama, Editions Phil Slivier, Paris, 1990

Howell, Georgina *In Vogue*, Condé Naste, 1991

Leymarie, Jean *Chanel*, Skira/Rizzoli, New York, 1987

Mackrell, Alice *Coco Chanel*, Batsford, London, 1992

Madsen, Axel *Coco Chanel, A Biography*, Bloomsbury, London, 1990

Marquand, Lilou *Chanel M'a dit*, Jean Claude Lattès, Paris, 1990

Morand, Paul *L'allure de Chanel*, Hermann, Paris, 1976

Mulvagh, Jane *Vogue History of Twentieth Century Fashion*, Viking, London, 1988

Spencer, Charles *Cecil Beaton: Stage & Film Design*, Academy Editions, London, 1975

Swanson, Gloria *Swanson on Swanson*, Random House, New York, 1980

Vreeland, Diana *DV*, Weidenfeld & Nicolson, London, 1984

Wilson, Elizabeth and Taylor, Lou *Through the Looking Glass*, BBC Publications, London, 1989

Exhibition Catalogues

Abbaye de Royallieu, Compiègne, France, *Tisserands de Légende, Chanel et le tissage en Picardie*, Eds ASPIV, 1993

Fine Arts Museum, Bunkamura, Tokyo *Mademoiselle Chanel*, 1990

Sale Catalogue

Christie's *Sale of the Personal Collection of Chanel*, London, December 1978

Article

Mount, Laura 'Designs on Hollywood', *Colliers* 4 April 1931

Magazines

Various issues of the following magazines have all provided useful source material. *Adam; Album du Figaro; Art, Gout, Beauté; l'Art de la Mode; Chiffons; Comoedia Illustrée; Les Elégances Parisiennes; Elle; Excelsior Modes; Femina; Femme Chic; Figaro Illustré; Good Housekeeping; Harper's Bazaar; Jardin des Modes; Minerva; Mode Chic; L'Illustration; l'Officiel de la Mode; Vogue* (UK, American and French editons); *Woman's Journal*

Picture Credits

Index